365 Days *Single*

Confessions of a Serial Monogamist

By Orlena Cain

Take your time—there's no rush to find love. Enjoy the ride.

Love, Orlena

This book is a personal memoir. It's a combination of facts about Orlena Cain's journey, however, names and identifying details have been changed to protect the privacy of individuals. Any resemblance to actual persons, living or dead, or actual events is purely coincidental. The reader should not consider this book anything other than a work of literature.

365 Days Single

Confessions of a Serial Monogamist

Copyright 2018 by Orlena Cain

Cover art by Kinderd Productions / Kali Willows

Editing by: Wizards in Publishing

All rights reserved. Except for use in any review which will be approved upon request, the reproduction or utilization of this work, in whole or in part, in any form by any electronic, mechanical, or other means now known or hereafter invented is forbidden without the written permission of the publisher.

Published by Orlena Cain

Look for her online at:

www.orlenacain.com

Acknowledgements

Life is a journey, not a race. It is a day-by-day adventure that brings with it beautiful opportunities, some in the form of friendships. Back when I was in public school, I had the good fortune of making a dear friend, Dr. Julie Gowthorpe. We remain connected to this day. I remember from the early years her kindness, and this is exactly who she continues to be to this day. My renewed friendship and conversations with her ignited some changes within me that have brought me closer to who I used to be and even more of who I always was supposed to be.

My other long-standing friendships have grown strong over the years with four other remarkable people; Jamie Godin, Darek Wierzbicki, Jody Bain and Erick Hiller. Growing up with the presence of a real father who represented love in a non-sexual way was something I never had the privilege of knowing. To be seen in the eyes of these incredible friends, not as a sexual possession, but as a human being with genuine needs, I was able to see my own reflection in a new light. One where for the first time, my worth was determined by sincere interactions, and not the requirement to compromise myself in order to earn it. These remarkable men taught me more about love in the absence of physical intimacy than I ever could have expected. Thank you for your support and friendship. I am a better person for having known you.

To my partner in crime, co-hosting on the radio for over nine years, Sean Kelly. Sean is a dedicated, single dad and overall hard-worker that exemplifies what it is to be a good man. He shows me kindness and remains a solid professional as we spend our mornings lighting up the airwaves together. Being his friend has given me a front row seat to how true fatherhood should be. It has been an eye-opening experience to see such devoted parenting.

Dedication

This book is dedicated to my Oma. Her beautiful, unconditional love was present from the beginning of my life till the end of hers last year. Oma was my saving grace. She rescued the slivers of my heart in the wake of trauma and kept my ability to love strong despite my past. Hers is a love that can never be replaced, yet in her passing, she managed to leave such a huge space for a new love to take root and grow. I miss her every day and hope that my courage to love as she did makes her happy wherever she may be.

Foreword

Sinking ourselves into relationships cannot—and will not erase the scars of the past. Instead, they add layers to them as they rot deep inside of us. No one asks to be traumatized, but so many of us have to survive among the ruins of the aftermath.

The damage shapes how we view the world and our place in it. It forces us to develop coping strategies to protect ourselves from further harm. Sometimes, these necessary defenses end up reinforcing the negative patterns engrained in our lives, to our detriment.

At the end of her first memoir, *Unlucky in Love: Confessions of a Die Hard Romantic*, Orlena Cain committed to spending 365 days single, while she rediscovered herself. This was done with the intent of healing the festering wounds she has hidden for a lifetime. Being single and dating with no commitment to a relationship sounded like a death sentence to her, but she realized it was down to *now or never* to wake up and really get to understand her inner demons—so that she can learn how to abolish them.

Join Orlena as she journeys through 365 days of personal discovery. This is not a story about romance, but one of self-healing, understanding, and improving one's life and pursuit of personal happiness.

My Life-Affirming Wake Up Call

In the epilogue of my first book, "Unlucky in Love: Confessions of a Die Hard Romantic," I drew some rather powerful conclusions about my experiences and my luck, or lack thereof, in my pursuit of happiness. If you haven't read it, I'd recommend you check it out to give you the background of the driving force in my ongoing journey to everlasting love. After soul searching and seeking feedback from some important people and resources, I was better equipped to recognize my lack of luck was a direct result of early childhood trauma and learned coping skills. I outlined my whirlwind of romantic endeavours and how I came to terms with the fact that the damage incurred had impacted my outlook on relationships and defined what I was drawn to in a really detrimental way.

It made me realize how I shifted from one relationship to another, focusing on potential partners and their happiness instead of healing the wounds of my past. The very ones that dictated my every decision.

At the end of my first memoir, I committed to spending 365 days single, while I rediscovered myself and worked on changing unhealthy patterns. I did this with the purpose of healing the festering wounds I've hidden for a lifetime. Being single and dating with no commitment to a relationship sounded like a death sentence. However, I had decided at this point, that if I didn't take a break from relationships, the next one might destroy my desire to ever have one again. It was down to now or never to wake up and really get to understand my inner demons—and learn how to abolish

365 Days Single

them.

One might think thirty-two years of endless dating 'would have made me feel like that at some point. It didn't. I could have likely kept dating forever. If there's one thing I know for sure about myself, it's that I hate to quit on anything. As it stood, the last relationship with "Poseur," mentioned in my first book, didn't end the way I anticipated. As I look back, deep down I knew it was going to end eventually. This last commitment was yet again, to another emotionally unavailable man. I just didn't think it would end in the disheartening way it did.

Things came to light so shocking that it only took me thirty minutes to pack his clothing in the containers that he'd brought them in, and slide them out to the elevator.

Something inside me had finally snapped, not just because of him and that particular situation, although it was a solid kick in the ass. Now, I can see my entire love life had finally come to the breaking point. Something had to change. I had to change.

It's not like he was actually living with me. He was a "weekend boyfriend." I couldn't handle having him around anymore than that. My physical attraction to him was the factor that kept me willing to work on it, but I could only enjoy his company in small amounts of time. I had to end the relationship. There are some boundaries that I will never tolerate being crossed.

It made me sad to find that Poseur was unable admit to himself who he really was, which, in itself is his own issue. In a relationship, however, with hidden truths uncovered, it turned out to be a show, an act, one designed to draw a person in, but not able to sustain it with any real substance. When you don't know who you really are deep down inside, how can you be with anyone else? You can't. It's that simple. So that's what made me turn on my heels and walk away, shutting down communication completely. It was my perception that he couldn't come to terms with who he really is, and accept that the unhealthy things about him negatively affected those around him, including me. He wasn't able to admit things needed to change if he wanted real happiness, which, in turn, he considered everyone else's fault.

True to my old patterns and way of existing, I focused my energy on supporting his attempts at personal growth, but I felt a familiar spiritual drag creep in. One I've become more aware of, one that never ends well for anyone. To gain my energy back, I blocked his number, removed him from social media, and erased any traces of him from my life. The hurt and negativity was more than I was willing to tolerate. I didn't want to be reminded of him in any way, and I didn't want to hear any more absurdities coming from his lips.

If you truly listen to your intuition, you can always feel lies deep inside. It's even worse when you discover hard-core proof of that treachery. Some of us who have been tempered by deceit and betrayal learn to listen to those haunting instincts. We know that feeling when someone lies to us. At some point, we're all guilty of it: white lies, small lies and even big lies. I can feel when someone lies because I get a numbness just under my ribcage that won't go away. It's my inner lie detector.

The reason I fell into this relationship in the first place was because of my previous heartbreak. The one that hurt me so bad it shattered my heart into a million splinters. My way of coping was to turn away from the devastating pain, or rather run. In fact, I ran smack into someone else's. In this case, it was better to deal with someone else's pain and heartbreak than my own. Something I

365 Days Single

concluded after I worked through this last failed attempt at finding love.

With the annihilation of this relationship, I only had one matter of business to tie up, and it wasn't with Poseur. It was with a ten-year-old. This incredible little person I made a bet with when this relationship first started. One of my best friends, Janine, who has been around through many relationships of mine and has laughed and cried along with me through them all, has two wonderful children: a lovely boy and a sweet little girl. Janine's firstborn, a girl, and I are very close. She loves me dearly, unconditionally. It's really quite beautiful, her sweet protection of me. To them both, I am Yaya, the fun and crazy aunt/one of her mom's best friends.

One day, shortly after Poseur and I started dating, Janine's daughter and I jokingly made a deal. I said to her, if this one does not work out, I will give you some money. She suggested twenty dollars, but I bumped it up to a hundred. I figured if it didn't work out, she'd have money for her education and I will have no doubt learned something more of myself, yet again. A more valuable lesson. Now, I can imagine what you're thinking about this exchange, a deal for money, with a kid? Really, Orlena? As odd as it sounds, this innocent, sweet little girl was holding me accountable for my relationship. Having seen me over the years not settled into a long-lasting love like her own mother, she acknowledged the lack of normalcy in my relationship endeavours. After all, the students often become the teachers.

The weekend following the breakup, I was invited to Toronto for Janine's fortieth birthday party, and I picked this moment to settle up. I would never break a promise or fall out on a deal, especially not to her. Even this young genius saw a pattern that wasn't serving my happiness. I arrived just prior to the event, and sat her down, told her the relationship was over, and handed over the cash. She waved the twenties around in front of me, beaming. I'm not sure if she was beaming from winning or happy I ended the relationship with Poseur. I never got the impression she was fond of him during our time together.

One particular issue she voiced discomfort with, was his inappropriate affection toward me in front of others. His boundaries were miniscule, and the innocence of childhood is so easily marred by these interactions. Physical intimacy should be kept private, not on display in front of others. Children are so observant and honest. When a child notices a person being constantly objectified, it impacts them. It sets a precedent for them in their learning about relationships and intimacy.

At her young age, she was able to see this exchange was inappropriate. There is a time and place for everything, but Poseur didn't seem to understand the need for these types of boundaries in the presence of other people. Nor did he seem to realize the impact it can have on their emotions. In my experience with him, this proved to be the majority of the problems he encountered. In retrospect, I'm thankful this is no longer an issue I need to concern myself with.

Once again, here I sit, single. This time around, I actually found it to be more freeing than I expected. I realized I was pretty emotionally uninvolved with Poseur. As I rule, I tend to keep my pace jam-packed with no real time to spare. Little did I know it was a coping skill I'd developed to distract myself from the scars I'd spent a lifetime trying to forget. I worked hard every day, doing double duty. Early morning radio hosting and then working at my

365 Days Single

store downtown in Belleville for most of the day kept me occupied throughout the week. Community gatherings and event planning, and hitting the hay at 8:00 p.m. doesn't leave you with a lot of downtime to look for true love. I had manufactured an extraordinarily busy life for myself and kept it going at warp speed the majority of the time.

After the conclusion of the relationship, I decided it was now or never to try things a different way for a change. I wasn't looking for love at this point and decided to renew my dedication to the pursuit of real happiness. This was new territory. I had come to terms that my goal didn't mean looking for love but rather for meaning. I needed to rediscover myself as an individual, and not how I'd fit into a life designed for his-and-her bath towels. My inner demons surfaced more frequently with each relationship, to the point they haunted my every waking thought. The idea of developing self-awareness gave me a new sense of purpose. I had drawn some powerful conclusions that sparked the inspiration for change.

Having belief in oneself is something I take very much to heart. Many of us lose that focus on our personal growth and development when we orchestrate so many other things to maintain a continuous barrier of distraction.

Growing up without the encouragement to believe in myself from my parents, I had to find my own way to achieve that. I decided it's crucial to take hold of who you are. Redefine what you believe in, what makes you real, dig deep and learn about who you really are, inside and out. Once you have it, never let it go. Once you believe in yourself, no one can take it from you. Life can throw whatever it will your way, and it won't matter. The trick is finding that belief, harvesting it, and holding it. You instill it in yourself, and it will stay put. Some mistake having a strong belief in oneself as ego or stubbornness. I've been called stubborn simply because I didn't want to do what someone else wanted, or they tried to sway me from my core values. I credit this determined disposition as the survival tool that pulled me through difficult times.

My Auntie-Ma and my Oma instilled such strength in me. They both encouraged me to be strong and persevere through my hardships and suffering. Some may convey that as obstinacy, but that's not how I see it. I found it served a purpose and helped me when I felt weak and vulnerable.

At this stage in my evolution of me, I feel revived and renewed. I'm not in a rush, nor am I looking for anyone to be paired up with. My life keeps me connected to the community and to people in general, so I don't find this new path lonely at all. I'm a highly social person. I put positive energy out there, and I absolutely love knowing people. I like to think the energy within me usually attracts people who are in need of the energy and enjoy the feeling. I just have to be more aware of the psychic vamps who zap your life force in a draining way.

It's a mindfulness I work at now to keep my space from negative dynamics that serve no healing purpose. Determining who is healthy to be around, who can soak up your shared energy, the genuine people who need your positivity, requires objectivity. Like a camel dying of thirst, people who drain you are always looking for a cool drink of your energy source. For the most part, my enthusiasm has attracted good men and women, and that's why I don't change. When those good people are around, the energy flows out and circles back around because they have positivity, too. The flow of power is good for everyone when it's good. It's a wonderful,

365 Days Single

symbiotic exchange we all thrive from.

Now that I am dedicated to being single for the first time, I wake up in the morning and sit down in front of my keyboard, drink coffee, and type. Reflecting on my thoughts and feelings, confident in the new clarity I've acquired feels so good. Sometimes, I write in the middle of the day or late at night, too. It feels good to draw focus to my own thoughts and not have to put out the emotional fires for someone else or be needed by them. I'm excited by this new goal because I am spending time with me, committed to me, and that feels incredible.

I'm not looking for anyone but my hidden self. For who I am and what this new me looks like. Getting to know my inner truths over the course of this year is my priority. Only after I accomplish this in full will I make any judgments or big decisions about what direction I should move in. Being a free spirit and just hanging around is so liberating. No pressure, no absurd deadlines or relationship goals. I pay my own bills, make my own choices, and pay attention to my close friends. I give back to my community by sharing my time with charitable organizations when I can, to build the positive vibes within. I have always felt fulfilled, whether if I had someone with me or not. However, I can see now how I often got sucked into the ideology that you should be paired up with someone because that seems to be what the world is conditioned to believe. Whoever will be in my future has to be able to just flow in and around it and not tax it with emotional drama and negative behaviour. Free-flow love.

Being single has not changed my day-to-day existence. I still go to bed and wake up just like before. Most women I know love going to bed and waking up to sweet messages from someone who likes or cares about them. Rather than relying on a man to provide this feel-good, I signed up to Daily Om which gives you daily inspirational messages of encouragement. It's actually quite lovely to wake up to positive messages that are inspiring and non-sexual. The positivity without personal cost is so much better for my mind and my focus.

My philosophy in getting to know people over this year of being single is to not cloud sexual attraction with compatibility beyond the sheets. Despite the anticipated spikes in the ole hormones from time-to time, I don't want to get to know anyone sexually. Sex confuses things, which is counter-intuitive to the whole 365 day plan.

Dating is my middle ground. Everyone needs contact and interaction. What I need is to take a step back from my norm of jumping headfirst into any more committed relationships for this entire calendar year. To be completely honest, I realize, I'm human with typical baser needs, a woman in her prime. Realistically, I might have to succumb to the odd primal urge here and there. If I can manage to avoid engaging with anyone in a way that leads me back to old patterns, it will improve my ability to better assess their fit. Dating without the muddled cloud of sex-confused intimacy overcasting my clarity of what a real relationship should evolve into. No diving into messy commitments where I try to please a partner and build something from nothing. Makes sense, doesn't it?

My reality is I'm single, with no children, and I can do whatever I please. Taking a year to learn, heal, and grow won't impact anyone else. I'm not responsible for anyone but me. With this as my starting point, I will spend this year as I choose and let it unfold as it may, but I will remain single. Whatever will happen is meant to be, and I'll face it with fortitude. It's not like I think some climatic finale will happen, but I pray I make it to the end with a greater understanding of what I want, and maybe even get as far as to figure out who I want that with. On the flip side, I may find being single is what I actually needed all along. Only time will tell, and I've given myself 365 days to sort it all out. For a serial monogamist with a track record of being alone for little to no time between relationships, this is essentially a lifetime for me.

As my days progress into this new way of living, the idea of checking out different people and not making any sudden moves is actually a relief. There's no pressure or timeline I have put on myself to find someone. Beginning from a lesson I learned long ago—you can't judge a book by its cover—I'll move forward one step at a time. I've come to terms with the fact that not everyone is who they appear to be. Everyone is different, from age to walks of life, looks, personalities, and professions. I'm not forming any opinions about anyone and keeping an open mind. I'm taking nothing seriously and keeping with my mandate of not getting involved with anyone.

It's also part of my goal during this year to avoid my tendency to pre-judge anyone or lead anyone to believe that I want anything serious. Old habits die hard. No. I have to remain neutral, but it is necessary to reset my compass. Get it into a neutral position, so that I can navigate my love life with better clarity. It's not easy for anyone, but now that I've had three major strikes to the heart in a row, I feel more apprehensive than ever. My marriage ended, my engagement broken, and a one-year, soul-sucking relationship were over, all within the last seven years.

The best thing about all that has transpired is that it inspired me to write my first memoir, *Unlucky in Love*. Over the course of writing my first book, I stumbled across an eye-opening breakthrough in my relationship patterns. Seeking professional support to work through my failed attempts at finding love, I came to terms with the discovery that I have an attachment disorder. A debilitating disorder, forged by the trauma of my abusive childhood and cemented into my adulthood. This new knowledge lurks in the back of my mind when I meet men. A great deal of soul-searching erupted after this. My approach to new love prospects is now shrouded with the lingering question; am I attracted to this person because they are bad or good for me?

This next year should be interesting, engaging, and eye-opening about who I am and what will work best with me, regardless of age, looks, or height. One factor I won't change my mind about in potential partners is that having a steady job is essential. There may be some people who don't have that as a determining factor for finding a partner. As I see it, it kind of goes without saying. You don't have to be a rich man for us ladies, but you have to have a steady income. No steady income...no steady anything. Be prepared for a universal response to you being single for any period of time.

As it stands, almost immediately after I made my proclamation of committing to 365 days of single, the universe started firing off a range of ages and types my way as a test, or at least that's how I feel. To see if I was really serious about my year study. There was a nice range of men to get a better understanding of not only what I like but what works best with me. Very funny, universe, very funny!

How did I manage to accumulate so much interest from many so men in such a little time? I was opening myself to a greater understanding and staying open without engagement. Be aware of who's around you. I'm not looking at my phone when I'm walking around this world. Instead I'm looking at what is around me to take

365 Days Single

it all in and enjoy the moment. It doesn't matter where I am, now, or what I'm doing. My brain is a clean slate, and my eyes are wide open when I'm looking at anyone.

Moments happen. Life should be taken in. Not always looking at people, places, or things as such a negative or positive experience, but perhaps considering it a learning experience. This is why the succession of my wide-awake moments led me to meet so many different men in so little time. I can only imagine what should lie ahead in the months to come. This flow had better slow down to a more moderate level, though, because I can barely keep up with the natural shift that needs to occur. I have a broad dating history that is going to benefit me in knowing what has not worked in the past and not repeating it. The marker for me will be when a relationship could have worked in the past, but I was just not in the right place at the right time. The other issue will be to balance what I have learned with what I was not ready for, what could have worked but may not work now based on my evolution. Yikes! This is going to be hell of an awakening in the year to come. I wish you luck if you feel the desire to embark on the same journey of self-discovery.

For those of you reading this for inspiration on a similar venture of self and redefining your love life, you have homework to do. Grab a journal and start writing down all your thoughts about the people you meet. It doesn't matter if they had a long conversation with you. Write down what you liked. What you didn't like. Hell, if that someone merely caught your eye at the dollar store, write down what you liked and why. The introspection when you read it later on will give you a world of insight. Trust when the answer is no, there will be a better answer down the road.

The Dance of Attraction

The magical moment real attraction happens is an unexplained phenomenon. Most people experience that kind of feeling when drawn to a potential love interest. You can't predict that moment or even divert the energy when it erupts. The sensation of attraction can either rip through your body like a lightning bolt or slip across your nervous system like a cool breeze. Either way, you can't ignore the feeling when it consumes you, nor can you stop it.

Attraction is instantaneous, or at least, that's the kind I tend to experience. You could be having a bad day, the worst day of all, or the greatest moment. When a star struck, potent attraction happens, it's like winning the lottery. Your numbers come up, and the music starts to play like on the 649 machine. "Winner, Gagnon!" I've felt this so many times, and I absolutely delight in the moment it rolls through me. Some might say, it's an addictive type of feel good because it's magical.

The most recent moment of this type of lightning bolt attraction happened at the oddest time and when I truly was not prepared for, nor looking for it. It was at one of my closest friend's birthday parties. She was throwing the bash at her beautiful home and I knew only her family and close friends would be there, most of whom I had met. So I had it in my head to go whoop it up with her, consume a lot of drinks, and get downright silly. This was in my head as I drove the few short hours to her place in Toronto. I had finally ended a one-year relationship that had long since been over, and I was finally able to breathe again and feel free. You know that feeling

365 Days Single

that lingers when you are trying to get out of a relationship? You feel like you are numb and just existing, and when finally out of it, you feel so new again.

My girlfriend knows how to throw a party, and when I arrived the band was just setting up inside. She'd planned an outdoor event, with cool lounging stations and intimate fires, but the rain would just not go away, so everything had to be rerouted. Even the ambient light strands that had been planned for outdoors had also been strung throughout the home to create a warm, hipster vibe. Cocktail stations were set up, and the chef was busy in the kitchen when I arrived. It was such a feel good evening. Lots of love at the celebration.

Turning forty is such a significant milestone, as it kind of marks your halfway point. It gives you a chance to look back and then forward at the same time. It's a moment in time when you can change anything for the positive because you should be wise enough and strong enough at that point to make adjustments if needed. My girlfriend needs none. She has the perfect life. Two healthy and beautiful children and a husband who has loved her dearly for the past sixteen years. So, on this evening, there was nothing but pure energy and positive vibes in the home, which is exactly what I needed to be immersed in.

The evening got underway with the band playing just about anything under the sun and lots of the birthday girl's favourites. Even the couple who formed the band together were engaged and getting married in a few weeks. They had met on a bus years before and called themselves the Greyhound Riders. How appropriate, I thought. All this lovely energy circulating around and in the midst of it all, friends, family, and...him. Who was this tall, cool glass of water who walked in with some family members? I had never seen this man before. Tall, lean, and possessed of a lovely mess of hair that all together made him pretty damn sexy. He wore plaid and, in the city, that's kind of hipster, but he wasn't being hipster at all. He was just being himself, I later found out.

Who was this guy? He was my friend's cousin, originally from up north and working in Toronto periodically with a business. I'd never heard of this cousin before, but I wanted to know him now. Let's call him Dunc. His deep-dark-brown eyes were warm and intriguing. Let the dance begin. Dunc was on one side of the room. On the other side, I stood, being casual and cool. The feeling brought me back to what it was like at a high school dance.

People danced and drank, as you do at a good party. I took him all in from afar. His smile was striking, his style and his soft approach to the way he spoke to people intriguing. The heat in the room grew intense, but I soon realized, it wasn't from the body heat of party goers, and not from the Edison lights either. The heat was the chemical response to the attraction that ignited throughout my body. This intensity surfaced and made itself known in the oddest of places.

At first, I tried to ignore it and convince myself it was something else. Maybe the vanilla whiskey I was drinking? As the night progressed, and the drinks began to flow, it was undeniable, it wasn't the whiskey. The pulse pounding behind my ears made it clear. I had a thing for this guy. Despite Dunc being charming and courteous, I had no inkling if he had any interest in me. Later in the evening, I took a chance, crossed the room, and broke into conversation with him. I held no expectation of what would come from talking to him, yet the attraction surged inside me when I was close to him.

It was the slowest I had ever moved against the emotion, but I had just broken up with someone and proclaimed that I would be single for a year. There was no way this first glance could pry me from my conviction. *I'm still holding myself to being single. No harm in window shopping. I just needed to remember, I'm not there to buy the goods.* The dance of eyes and minor flirtatious comments circled between us over the course of an hour.

The night continued, many socializing intermittently between us, music swirled around us, and there was a chemistry brewing, although it was subtle. Soon, the evening came to an end. People began to file out, and there we were sitting on the couch next to each other chatting. It was just me and him. I didn't care for a moment who was around, but in the back of my mind, I was wondering what my girlfriend would say.

Yet that damn attraction is a lot like that heated rush from alcohol. Its effects are unpredictable, as are your inhibitions when it pumps through your veins. I tried to be cool, but those eyes, those damn deep, dark, beautiful eyes lured me to him. I never thought I would be kissing her cousin at the end of her birthday party, but there we were, lips pressed against one another. It was brief and powerful. It was disorienting, momentarily, and I had to gain back the strength of my senses and return to reality. These types of encounters can linger just long enough to have an effect on you a few days later.

The seduction swirled around me one evening, and when it touched down in the form of a kiss, it was undeniably real, and I couldn't resist the moment of bliss. We exchanged numbers and texted a little after he went back to his hometown, and soon our connection sort of fizzled out. I stopped messaging him, and he didn't initiate texting me back. That's okay with me. Sometimes you just dance a few songs of romance, and that's it. It is still a wonderful memory and a strong slap in the face from my inner voice, telling me that we were on a mission and this was a bold diversion to test me. I almost failed this test by allowing my thoughts start to wander as they tend to.

Thinking of how this person could fit in my life. Could I visit him up north? Would he be able to come down here? Like an alcoholic coming off the hooch cold turkey, I stopped myself dead in my tracks because I knew I was far from ready for anything. A rule of thumb I reminded myself of is men will go after what they want. It's their instinct, and they will not pursue something that they don't want or who they feel they can get and keep. Don't try and convince yourself otherwise. If only more men and women could wrap their head around this truth.

Maybe it's our fragile egos and damaged self-esteem that allow us to play this mind game with ourselves. God forbid if someone genuinely just wasn't into you—get over yourself. Honestly, I am preaching to the choir. It is a difficult task to achieve, but the time you are wasting convincing yourself of a connection that most likely does not exist or has expired, is time you could be using for yourself.

Here's the lesson I took from this experience:

You don't have to get involved with every person you meet and have a connection with. Sometimes you can just let things be as they may and since I never really pushed or pursued the situation, it just faded. Don't try or push too hard with someone who is clearly not into having a relationship and doesn't make any attempt to stay connected. It only leads to angst, disappointment, and frustration.

365 Days Single

Furthermore, if you're at a spot where you're cleansing your palate from relationships, it's not going to come this quick or easy. You should be focused on you and only you. Look at these temptations as something to take in, understand, and move on with that understanding. At this point in my journey, I reminded myself of my past patterns and behaviour and although it was difficult to drop the idea of Dunc, it had to be slam dunked. *Boom*. Moving on.

Looking Back to Move Forward

I spent the month of May in reflection. Reflection is always a good thing. As long as you don't linger too long looking back, and you do it without harsh judgment of yourself or others. Accept the experiences you've had, regardless of the outcome, be it positive or negative, with the purpose of giving you a greater understanding of yourself.

Keep looking forward. I typically don't like to look back, but in this case, I felt in order to understand what would not work, I had to reassess the events of my past. There's an unspoken rule I have for myself: never speak to anyone I've dated after the relationship ends. Once it's over, I feel that's it, and I choose to move on. There is no point in rehashing old wounds. Everyone has their own rules on how to navigate dating; this one had worked. Especially if it didn't end well.

As I've gotten older, though, I am less militant about it. Meaning, if I bump into someone or they seek me out, I won't be rude. Sometimes, the reasons for reconnection are not about starting a relationship up again, but rather to get closure, for one or both people. The particular situation or how long ago the breakup was is the determining factor. I definitely do not, have not, and will not become someone's best friend after a relationship is over.

For some reason, as of late, some men from my previous dating experiences have tried to reconnect with me via social media or good old-fashioned text. It seems strange that when I proclaim I'm going to be single for a year, men start popping up all over. Is it a trend, or

365 Days Single

am I just suddenly more aware of it? As I said before, it's my belief this theme is a universal response. I'm going to take it as a helping step to clear up old wounds and get the closure I never sought before so I can grow and move closer to finding true love. Taking it for what it all is and investigating it without any suspicion or expectation is a little bending of my original rule. I'll accept on this learning curve.

As for old connections reaching out, I typically never delete phone numbers because you never know when you are going to need that contact for a reason other than a relationship. The only time I erase all potential for contact is if the person truly burnt their bridge with me forever. Betrayal of trust would burn it down for good. For that reason, if someone reaches out and says, "You probably won't remember me," they would be entirely wrong. I do, because I have their phone number. Although the days gone by when my contacts were contained in my little black book, those of course have been long gone for years. Even so, I consider everything is as it should be.

One reconnection I did explore was with My Private Eye (from the first book). He had previously reached out and offered to have coffee or lunch sometime if I was in Toronto. One day, by chance, I had time to catch up with him. I contacted him and he invited me to visit him at his new house, since he'd sold the one we had owned together a few months prior. This new place was a fresh start for him out on his own. Not one he had bought with a woman who broke his heart. I was curious why he wanted to talk and would never think it was because of any love interest.

There was a nasty storm on the day we actually could meet. I was shopping at a Costco in his area and texted him. When it was time to leave to meet him, I was met with a torrential downpour and got trapped just inside the building doors with a group of other people. It struck me as symbolic that I had to wait for the storm to pass before I could leave. Shocker. I messaged him and told him I would be delayed and he joked that if I was soaking wet, he could dry my clothes.

Although it was a cute offer, I chose to wait for the skies to clear. I was clear on my agenda, but I got the impression old habits die hard, and maybe the flirty message indicated he still had some sort of physical desire for me. With no interest in wavering, my rule of not rehashing old relationships held me true to my conviction. I was in control of what would or wouldn't happen. None of "that" was on the docket, not at all. It never even took a split second of reconsideration. I didn't feel the same way about him as I had years ago.

My visit was brief and purposeful. I stopped in for a hello and a drink. It was pleasant to find he was still very much the sweet and hospitable guy I once knew. There was no awkward tension. Instead, he hugged me and stole a few quick pecks on my cheek. Relief washed over me when he ended it there with no attempts to cross physical boundaries. It was important in my mind that we keep things friendly and neutral. I wanted to see if I could and how would it feel to hang out with an ex on a friendly level.

It felt weird, which reinforced why I don't do this in the first place. After our visit, I wondered what reconnecting with him would do in the greater scheme of things. It was my hope it would help heal a bad breakup for us both, and mend the heart I was responsible for breaking. Even though he was willing to leave things on a neutral level, I considered maybe that peaceful resolve would help heal the wound and we would both benefit from the closure.

Since then, we've talked a few times and exchanged texts. The reconnect may have left a different impression for him than I hoped, as P.I. suggested we go out for dinner or away for a night. A night away? Treading familiar territory once again, even as friends, this didn't strike me as a healthy idea. I'm not sure where I am with my own healing. This created a cloud of confusion and left me uncertain about what I want to do. To try and picture us back together at some point didn't feel right. The past was gone, and my old rule stayed true. We'd had our time, and it wasn't meant to be. My intent was to develop a clear understanding of what I learned about myself and where was I now.

 Overall, this was a therapeutic step and did provide the closure I needed. I was able to embrace the knowledge that once the love is gone, so is the connection, and when the connection is gone, so is the friendship. It would always have a subtle weirdness to it, and a future partner for either of us probably wouldn't like the connection, especially since we don't share children together and there is no reason to connect.

 If you're offered a chance to make something right, and it is so easy to do so, you really should take the time to do it. It's not often we get the chance to heal old wounds or seek the closure we deny ourselves in the heat of a terrible moment, but I'm glad I made the effort to make it so this time. I can honestly say, that he is still a good person at heart. Our time has passed, what once was, is no longer, and I'm okay with that. I got the impression he was, too.

 During the course of the month, I thought about what I wanted to learn from this year of reflection. How I wanted to chart the new and improved course of this dating adventure. Dating without commitment. Something else I drew a firm conclusion about was my determination I would not be dating locally. There are not enough fish in the sea in my home town that I can connect with or have anything in common with. My profession as a media broadcaster puts me in a fishbowl of sorts, and men don't want to end up a topic of conversation on the radio. Others can't relate to my strong, upfront personality because I say what I mean with no holds barred. Some have shared that they feel for those reasons, I'm not real in some ways. I am 100 percent real.

Nonetheless, I wouldn't completely rule out a local love prospect who wanted to go out for dinner or coffee. Nothing ventured, nothing gained. That's what this whole process of remaining single is supposed to give me. Insight into the mechanics of dating and past mindsets and approaches that didn't work out.

In another attempt to better understand where love went wrong, I reached out to a person who meant a great deal to me in the past, Karlof, mentioned in the first book, who still lived in Germany. It provided me with new insight from my failed love history. To look back at this sad ending would allow me to see clearly ahead and better comprehend who I was then and who I am now.

Karlof and I had a good connection back then. In fact, it was pretty intense, although short lived. I reached out to him once when I was in my thirties after not seeing him for so long and cleared the air. Yes, I did bend my own rule, but he was different from the others. When we spoke last, I was sad to discover he was in the middle of a divorce. In his own efforts to move past a broken heart, he was starting to date someone new. It didn't strike me at the ideal time to ask some questions about how we ended up the way we did or what had happened to him since then.

After allowing time for him to settle into his new life, I spoke to him once again this past year to see how things had changed for him

365 Days Single

and how things had developed for him. Unfortunately for Karlof, he was in the middle of another chaotic space. Sad for his circumstances, I soon wondered how I would know or sense this. When you are once so deeply connected to someone and in love, can you, years later, still sense things about them? I'd noticed his social media feeds were pretty quiet until recently. In his public sharing, there were no posts of his children or his new wife. If everything was going so well, wouldn't he showcase it a bit? Our feeds are filled with photos of glorious meals, kids off to school, summer vacations, and such.

I remembered this was always the difference between us. He is a private person, and I prefer sharing happy moments to encourage positivity in the world. He was always skeptical of letting anyone know too much. In hindsight, there might be some wisdom in this thinking. When we spoke, he was reaping the benefits of his dedication to his growing business and that everything was good in his second marriage. He was too busy to keep things updated and was just living. My heart did flutter when we spoke, and I was replaying memories in my brain, wondering if there would ever be a chance for us again. It was so long ago though.

A few questions I asked gave me insight. I asked how it felt for us to speak again, and if he felt I had changed or if there was anything we could have done differently in the past to salvage what we'd tried to build. Karlof offered the point of view that we were just kids back then, and we were all grown up now. His response seemed sincere. I didn't detect any hurt or defensiveness, not even a little anger. Karlof had let go of the past and that may have been the release I needed to move forward myself. Let's be real, in my first book, when I told this story, the lingering sadness of this love lost hadn't left me. There may have been remnant of guilt on my part that I couldn't be what he wanted in a partner. We wished each other well, and that was that.

After I processed our talk, I realized the hurt we both suffered at the end had healed, the scars had faded, and we had both moved on emotionally. The feelings we had were over, and this chapter for us was officially closed, and I was at peace with this discovery. There will always be a soft spot in my heart for him and the time we shared, but that time was long gone, and we are both different people now.

Funny enough, not long after Karlof and I spoke, someone I dated shortly after him happened to reach out. I was somewhat caught off guard but not surprised because it was just the continuing theme this year seemed destined to bring.

The arrival of this next ghost didn't revive sweet memories at all. It brought back flashes of unpleasantness I had gladly washed away. A few weeks prior, when he'd friended me on, Facebook, I was shocked but accepted the request so he could see I was doing well.

It stunned me even more when he showed up one day in my store, shortly before I sold it. The former prison guard mentioned in book one who cheated on me, not once, not twice but three times in one week while he was on vacation, thought he would like to see me again. For what reason? Why now? The idea of healing old hurts is important in my quest, but this ghost's presence shook the past hurts and stirred up some unresolved anger.

The nagging question that sparked in the back of my brain with this visit was why do the majority of people reach out to past loves? Sure, some may try to apologize for past behaviours and make amends, myself included. My intent is personal growth and healing.

365 Days Single

These types of ghosts, more often than not will materialize because they have been hit with a breakup or divorce and they, too, are searching for who they once were and who they are now. No other reason really makes sense.

This story has quite a twist. The very guy who hurt and betrayed me walked right into my store. But what had happened to the slicked-down muscular body that made the ladies swoon in his very presence? The man who stood before me had lost the physique that had made it so easy for him to play the field back in the day. Although he had done something about the hair loss situation he had going on back then.

My first response was to tell him to buy something and move on. Instead, I made him a coffee and sat down to have a chat. This was the first time I had seen him since I left our apartment in the middle of the night. I'm a mature woman who has her head about her and knew I was clearly not emotionally engaged in this situation. I figured there was no harm in hearing what someone has to say about what happened so many years ago. He was "fresh out of a marriage," and that's a scary place for anyone to be. Your identity is so tied up in one person—or family, if you have one, for so long that you don't know exactly who you are after it's all over. You face a point where you've worn so many different hats, and the one you have left for yourself has gone missing.

Curiosity got the best of me. I wanted to see if he'd outgrown his cheating ways and changed into a better version of himself. As he sat there in front of me, I thought back to who I was when I last saw him and it hit me, the universe had manifested another opportunity to further my personal insight into my past.

In our time together, I was a young woman who had no real

identity. A woman who was looking to validate who she was in what men thought of her. Constantly people pleasing and not really knowing who I was, led me to men who were not always the best choice.

This person was one of those guys. I'm a totally different person now. I have a career as a radio and television broadcaster; I owned a store, I had become a published author and event planner. I've accomplished so much and was on a journey of self-discovery. Mindful of my present state, I drank coffee with the man who'd broke my trust, crushed my heart, and added to my insecurities. Having grown out of the broken girl he knew, I was not going to stoop to a lower level and not honour another person's apology. If he planned to.

We both recounted the events leading up to and the day we parted ways, and we had very different perceptions of the events that had unfolded. Mine was concise: he cheated on me. This was concrete, solid, proven evidence which was why I left in the middle of the night. He didn't dispute it back then, however, his take on the events had been diluted over time. But his take on what happened was no longer relevant. I had no interest in rehashing the painful memories. The pressing issue during this exchange was to see if he would actually apologize for what happened. As it turned out, he did. Customers had come into the store, and I excused myself to tend to them, and he left.

Later that day he messaged me.

Casanova: *It was great to see you today and catch up. Don't fall in love with me again. I'm sure I couldn't handle you anyway, lol.*

No, mister, you could not, and I would not fall in love with you

365 Days Single

again. Once bitten, twice shy. It didn't deter him from asking me out again when I was visiting his city.

Me: *You're hilarious.*

Casanova: *Why? Are you laughing because you wouldn't date me again? Like you said when we talked, we were kids. I wanted to see you today to see how I'd feel. Same emotions flooded back. I felt like I was blushing the whole time. Don't get me wrong. I'm not looking to get into a relationship with you. It would be nice to hangout and catch up some more. Seems like you may have some interesting stories.*

Did I ever. They have driven me in a direction far, far away from the young woman of twenty-three you knew so long ago. I'm forty-six now. I wanted to be kind in my response, thoughtful and mindful of my words.

Me: *Thank you for the message and the quick visit. It is always nice to see where we were and where we are in life. Where I am right now does not involve reacquainting myself with past loves. Especially when the love ended in such a sad and painful way. We were kids, for sure, and that's all water under the bridge. However, it's been twenty-three years and although I can be "friendly" with you, that's where it ends. What happened between us was so long ago. There were some fun moments, but, again, the reasons for our relationship ending abruptly were not the nicest and definitely left a lasting impression on me. I wish you the best, and take care on your new journey outside of your marriage. Be good!*

When you are at a point of introspection, it's no wonder you start bumping into old loves or reconnecting in some way. It's like the universe is sending you a blessing in the form of an opportunity to reflect on the past you and how you may have changed.

While on my book tour for my first story, I bumped into a man I dated shortly after I survived a scary time with a guy I called Muzak. Those of you who read my first book may remember that was not a good time for me. If you can't remember why, I'll just briefly add it involved a traumatic experience of life and death, one I narrowly escaped. One that I carried with me for a long time. Muzak was not exactly an ideal relationship, and I was very scattered and disorganized at the time, which was opposite of my personal character.

How the hell could I emotionally connect with anyone after being traumatized like that? I couldn't. I never should have continued dating back then either. Yet, I can see so clearly now that I lived with fierce determination and force and never let anything slow me down, not even my brush with death.

This particular guy, Tryon, who I dated after my traumatic episode, Tryon was not in a great place either, which is why we ended up connecting. That piece of information didn't rush back right away, though, because so much time had passed. He refreshed my memory when I saw him that day. We were ultimately two broken pieces who didn't fit together. We were both reeling from recent break-ups. That's not a good thing. He was looking for fun, and I was looking for nothing. Although, for some reason, he thought I was on the same kick he was. I never was. I guess I had become really good at creating the illusion that made men feel closer to me than was actually possible.

Tryon had seen in a LinkedIn post that I was going to be in an area near him for a book signing and just showed up. I was stunned, because I hadn't seen him since in almost twenty years. We just drifted apart and in fact, I barely remember anything about dating him, which makes me sad. Despite my lack of recall until he mentioned a few things that brought me back to that time, he was sweet and supportive of my new endeavours. Tryon bought a book, said some kind things, and suggested we go for a coffee sometime, but I think we both were able to see there was no spark, and my rule of not rehashing fit this reunion. It was never meant to be, and I was okay with that. My new motto: Leave it where you found it, and that is where it is. I wish Tryon the very best.

Lesson: Remember when you are journaling for yourself and trying to make sense of why certain things are happening, you may not understand why and should just write down the events as they happen. Encounters sometimes make more sense as time moves along. You should expect the flood gates to open up with the purpose of cleansing all that is good and bad from your life. It was a natural progression, and it was a good thing. Just keep writing your feelings, predictions, and worries down. It will all make sense later.

Hard Habits to Break

The universe and your soul will hear what you say to them, and they will collaborate with you if you are ready to deal with what it is you say you want. The resulting experiences will also test you to see if you have learned the lessons of love you need to before you get to the good stuff you want.

Over time, I felt the universe was in the process of empowering me through the next phase of tests. I had such a distorted view of love and was disillusioned by how elusive it was. I seriously watch way too many romantic and romantic-comedy movies, including every one of Nicholas Sparks'. You cannot be a true romantic if you are not a card-carrying, movie-loving addict.

Just like a Nicholas Sparks scenario, on a warm summer breeze, a guy who looked just like Matt Damon wandered into my store in downtown Belleville. He sauntered in ever so slowly with this big, toothy smile. I thought, this guy looks familiar, and then it hit me, he looked like the P.I. I dated, only a smaller version, and perhaps a bit more like Matt Damon. I had been contemplating selling my store at the end of the year after some intense soul-searching. Realizing I was just too connected to the world, I came to terms with needing to unplug in order to look inward.

My store had always kept me busy outside of the radio station gig, but I was growing tired of it after the two years I spent pouring my heart and soul into it. I loved the people who shopped there regularly, but the wandering men who came in to try and pick me up drained my personal energy. The continuous pattern of feeling

365 Days Single

objectified by perfect strangers for nothing more than my appearance eroded my soul. Especially the ones who hardly bought anything. I had a clear-cut goal to sell things, not for my business to be utilized as a pick-up joint. Not a stage to prance around on in hopes of landing a man.

By the time he reached the cash register I was already calculating what was going to happen based on the feel of his energy.

"Have you been in before?" I inquired, as I always do if I did not recognize a potential customer.

"The beautiful smell drew me in, and now I can see why," he replied and smiled.

Oh, a charmer. Here we go and a dance of words and suggestive glances ensued. He picked up a few things after I gave him the nickel tour of the store and asked if there was anything else.

"Your phone number," he remarked.

This was exactly what I anticipated he would lead up to, and I wasn't swooned by the notion. Handing out my number was not an action I was interested in pursuing, but my morbid curiosity kicked in, and I caved. Yup, old habits die hard. I wondered what he would say outside the store. Did he have any kind of comprehension of how to speak to me like a real person, and not some object he was aiming for? Since this guy looked so much like Matt Damon, let's call him Matt.

Matt was new in town and didn't know anyone. His work had brought him here, and he wasn't sure how long he wanted to stay. Over the next few weeks, Matt would message me adoring things and stop in to drop a coffee off, even though I had a coffee machine. He was playfully flirtatious and youthfully alluring. He asked me to go for walks along the trail after I closed the shop. Ironically, going for a walk on the path was something I'd never done the whole time I owned this store. It was usual to be so exhausted every day after working double duty that I just wanted to go home. But it was summertime, and I allowed him to talk me into a stroll along the beautiful flowing river.

A few times over the course of the maybe two months we spent together, he invited me to his place for dinner. Casual and cool, like good friends hanging out. I really enjoyed being able to do that with someone with no strings attached. I had no interest in sleeping with him at all, so that pressure was relieved because he didn't push the topic. He was a really down-to-earth and sweet guy, and he reminded me of a when I was a teenager and found out someone had a crush on me.

It's those really natural and genuine feelings someone has for you when you are so young, all you have to offer to them is yourself. They aren't into you for your profession, or how much money you're making because chances are it's minimum wage, just like them. When you're young and have nothing more than maybe a cool car, you get a truer sense of why you actually like someone. Not much to judge or grade them on, but this slowly grows as we get older.

We women ask each other questions. What does he do for a living? How much money does he make? What kind of a house does he have? All of these extraneous things that don't make you get along any better together. Yet we continue to think this way, fantasize about this magical fairy-tale guy who we think exists to create this love we think will make us happy.

It doesn't seem to be that easy, and the long-time running TV shows *The Bachelor* and *The Bachelorette* proves this. Men and women line up to compete for one person against another twenty people in order to be the chosen one. They tolerate that one person kissing other people, flirting and connecting with other people right in front of them but have a whole series of rules about dating them in the real world. *The Bachelor or Bachelorette* whisk the contestants all around the world to different exotic locations for lavish dates and they fall for it hook, line, and sinker. Their logic is clouded by materialistic influences that do not actually mean you like the person or can get along any better with them in the real world.

    Anyone can fall for someone who showers them with all that money, attention, and romance. Nine times out of ten, the emotion does not sustain itself after the lights and cameras stop rolling. Just like in the real-life dating world. Which brings me back to the lesson I learned from hanging out with someone who was just a sweet and adorable person. Our time together taught me to acknowledge the things we should all appreciate in each other.

    After that person, I felt like a sitting duck in the store, just working away, and literally anyone could wander in and try and pick me up. I didn't like it at all, and the substance was just not there. I could not leave this journey to chance, and I needed to have access to more content.

    So, I did what everyone who is single does these days, I joined Tinder. Why not? Leonardo DiCaprio, Chelsea Handler, and other celebrities are on it, so there is no shame in the name of a good story. You may think I'm crazy for trying the online dating route, but I wanted to dig deeper into my understanding of what kind of love I wanted and what kind of person would bring it to me.

Love is the motivating factor for most people to connect with others. How do you find it beyond the smoke and mirrors? It looks like one thing but really evolves into something else and what the movies put makes my heart go pitter patter. Yet, this is an illusion I need to put to rest.

Love make influential men weak and successful women lose their common sense temporarily or forever. It's like a drug. If only love could be bottled and sold to everyone, versus scraping up whatever you can. If love came in a bottle form, ready for the consumer, it would have to have a lengthy warning label.

Warning, *this emotion may cause confusion, blurred vision, difficulty hearing, insanity, stupidity, loss of income, and delusional thinking.*

When you think about it, if love does all those things to you, then why would you even want it? Can you imagine for a moment, if it was in pill form. Would you take it? Every day you could just pop the Love Pill along with your vitamin C and magnesium before heading out the door. The euphoria that would sweep over you leaving your body tingling and warm. Would it become your morning ritual? Would your partner remind you to take it? Maybe they would leave it right next to your glass of orange juice on the kitchen table.

On days your partner really pisses you off, would you throw the pills down the toilet or hide them? *That's it, I'll teach 'em! I don't want any of that stupid love today, and they aren't getting any of it either! I want to feel anger and sadness instead. Won't that be fun?* All that fighting, bickering and lack of sex from not having the Love Pill. Who would do that? Because that's what happens when there is no love in your life. You feel empty and like something is missing

365 Days Single

from within.

Why would you lurk around all day with a dark cloud hanging over you when you could feel the bubbly, effervescent effects that love makes you feel inside? This is probably why I love drinking champagne so much. But, then again, I have done some really outrageous things when I have been hopped up on the bubbly stuff. Like, stripped down to my bra and underwear and made a snow angel outside when it was twenty below. No worries. I didn't feel the effects of the cold. I did, however, feel the effects of a headache though the next day and a mild snow burns on my backside. All worth it! Just like love.

The flip side of not taking the Love Pill would be if you took too much. Oh boy, I know what that feels like. Like when you first meet someone and everything looks, smells, and sounds like them. Your head spins and you feel like you are on drugs and you are, it's called Love.

Bye bye Matt Damon lookalike. Damon is not well known for his romantic movies anyway. This first brush with a tempting offer made me feel like I was vulnerable to love's persuasive skills still. It was the actually the opposite. In another time and place, I may have made it into something it was not. This time I took it as just another moment to teach me a lesson that I had already learned a long time ago.

Lesson: If you are a serial dater, like me, you will look for reasons to be with someone, because it is your natural instinct to do this. It's a bad habit that will be hard to break right away. If you have perpetually been in one relationship after another, you have the ability to look for the good in someone and overlook things you don't want to see. In this case, it is not a good thing. When you get into a relationship, it is a good thing to not sweat the small stuff, but when you're trying to break the pattern of finding commonality when there is very little to work with, this will be tricky. Waiting it out will allow you to have a clearer perception, and it won't be clouded by your bad habit or drawing comparisons. Not everyone who comes into your circle has the right to stay there. The old cliché is true. Some people are a reason, season, or a lifetime, but in this case, everyone is a reason to teach me something about myself. Using my store as a metaphor, sometimes, you come visit, purchase, and leave. That is the symbolic way that Matt entered my life and left it.

Summer Flings and Those Such Things

The month of May quickly turned into June, and summer was looming on the horizon. This time of year always carries with it such a feeling of newness. The shift of spring into summer, brings blossoms, growth, and change in the scenery, similar to what was happening within me. I felt different this summer. Normally, when the sunny season approached, I would be excited about sun tans and prospects of romance if I was not already in a relationship. If I was in a relationship, I would be looking forward to trips, vacations, family get-togethers with his family or mine.

Summer barbecues and party invites were always plentiful. This year, however, none of that was in the forefront of my mind. Instead, I was looking forward to the release of my book and for once, the focus was solely on me. What I had worked so hard over the past year and a half was about to bloom. Nothing was going to deter me from this. Besides, what guy in his right mind would want to start dating a woman who had a book coming out called *Unlucky in Love: Confessions of a Die Hard Romantic*?

Anyone I had mentioned it to previously laughed at the title and asked why I was so unlucky? "Good question," I would always say. On top of all that, my conviction to remain single for a year was strong within me, and there was no way I would allow myself to commit to anyone under any circumstances. After all, I had a plan for the entire calendar year. I was focused on me and nothing would divert my focus.

On a cognitive level, I was surefooted and moving full-steam ahead. A small part of me, however still required convincing and reminders of my dedication. It's like two forces battling inside, one saying, "Let me just see if this is feasible," and the other saying, "Oh, life is short. Go ahead and keep doing what you do." Only this time, I wasn't playing both sides. I was playing one side and that was the side that always kept losing. I wanted to win, so I went against my natural inclination and did the opposite of what I always had done before. As uncomfortable as that was, I pushed on.

I've heard some talk about being alone for long periods of time and not by choice, but rather lack of options. Their focus was on finding a partner. The thought of giving up on seeking that potential match seemed crazy to them.

Vowing to be single for a year could be an easier task if I kept my head down and went about my day-to-day existence with as much avoidance as possible. In *Eat Pray Love*, Author Elizabeth Gilbert ventured off to different countries to find herself. A beautiful notion, but that's not possible for all of us. We have to find ourselves in the modern world with family responsibilities, demands of work, and priorities.

For someone like me, who lives in the public eye and is constantly communicating with people, saying no thank you in a non-offensive manner becomes a constant chore. I think many of us need to learn to be able to say no thank you to offers and not feel responsible for how it affects others, keeping in mind that you are not responsible for anyone but yourself. What you do for you doesn't make you a bad person. This thinking might help to keep it all in perspective. Mindfulness.

You are only in control of the here and the now. Nothing else. My daily routine consists of balancing my time as a morning radio show host, store owner and party planner. All three require me to be in constant circulation, which puts you out there. I also am the type of person who lives a large portion of my career and my personal life on social media. Why? Contrary to popular belief, it's not for constant attention, but rather to keep constant attention on the people I am connected to. The more people who know me, the more who will tune into the radio station, shop in my store and come to my parties. It's a symbiotic existence to be a public figure and make it work. It helps that I enjoy knowing people over all. Connecting and sharing with people who want to be connected to you is not a bad thing in my mind. Since haters love to be connected and negative, I just wean them and screen them. Do the same. I readily admit it's easier said than done.

Connections with women are the easy part of my every day, because there is no expectation of anything further than friends, but with men there tend to be strings attached. Sometimes men misinterpret social media connections with more bountiful possibilities. If they observe no photos of a special guy on my feeds, it doesn't mean I'm looking for one.

It has become clear over recent years, and not just to me, that social media accounts seem to be shifting to the new pick-up spots for guys looking for a quick fix in finding sex. Not bars or the gym anymore. Loads of propositions come in through private messages suggesting get-togethers and more.

Somehow, this generation of tech-savvy people have completely overlooked the original intent of social media—making social connections—and see it as a private shopping gallery for eye candy and easy lays. Let's not forget the occasional marriage proposal from out-of-country people looking to settle into a new land with a ready-

365 Days Single

made life. It doesn't matter if you list your relationship status as single, married, or not searching for anything but friendship. My married friends get hit on by online trolls all the time.

How did this become a thing? It's even worse than spam. What happened to the idea of dinner dates or going to the movies and having popcorn? The instant gratification spurns greedy self-indulgent pursuits because they like a picture they see? How disappointing it must be for them to realize how many of these great pictures are manufactured or filtered into something unrealistic.

This turn of events makes my journey a more complex one, that's for sure. I liken it to a drug addict who is trying to stay away from drugs, but people keep knocking on your door offering it to you, and finding you everywhere you go. Men have been a constant and for no other reason than I thought I was supposed to keep searching till I found the right one. It's been exhausting while trying to attain my goals. Beginning and ending so many relationships is time-consuming, and if I had shifted my focus, maybe I would have become a doctor. I felt totally unfulfilled. I became so accustomed to having a man in my life that I always just had one and if I didn't, people would always ask why I was single. They would say, "You are so beautiful. Why can you not find someone?" or "Don't worry, you will find someone one day." On the other hand, when I had a boyfriend, people would offer, "You are so lucky," or "That's wonderful that you have love in your life." I would think, do I? Is it? Am I happy?

The truth is, deep down there has always been an empty longing I was never able to fully quench. Like I was not fulfilling my calling and instead I was tending to everyone else's. Making others' happy gave me purpose, but also proved to be my undoing. It became an unhealthy existence that I could no longer keep up. Change had to happen and I needed to grow past this incomplete person I've become. All this time, I've only tapped into a fraction of my potential for genuine happiness and my inner demons were about to be cast out for good. Whoever I was destined to grow into before all the horrible things started happening at the age of four, is who I needed to find again. That was so long ago, but the more work I do, the closer I feel myself getting to find that person.

So, I vowed to be single, and not commit to anyone until I found that person I'm truly meant to be. I will date, with the purpose of redefining who I for myself, who I will be as an individual first and not as a piece of a couple. A conscious decision to explore and not fall into the pattern I'm naturally inclined to of serial monogamy. My usual go-to of meeting a man, going on a few dates, like enough things about them to step up to physical intimacy and then have a relationship to get to know them. My norm…and that has been all goddam wrong.

The way it should go is the complete opposite of what I've been doing. If I had realized this sooner and had been wise enough to resist my natural inclination to jump into a relationship, I'd probably be a lot further ahead in knowing more about myself and the path I needed to follow to find myself.

Birthdays and Books

The months were creeping up to the release of my first book. I decided to do a soft release in August with the official release on my birthday in September. I love celebrating birthdays, and this gave me an even better reason to celebrate my birth with the birth of my book. Side note: when you were an unplanned pregnancy, proposed to be aborted and then set to be adopted...it's my deliberate goal to enjoy every day I'm here when there was a possibility I never would have been. That compiled with the childhood I had... I love the feeling of being alive and I do not take it for granted. Neither should you.

Don't let anyone tell you celebrating you being born is attention seeking or self-indulgent—you are a reason to celebrate. Take the day you were given to enter this world and stand at the top of a mountain, or on your balcony if that's all you've got, and scream, "I am here!" Your past year of being here taught you many things, good and bad, so take it all in.

With that being said, I had a birthday party/book release to plan and I needed a publicist. I found one locally who was fresh out of college with a ton of publishing experience. I was looking for someone ready to work, and she fit the criteria. Enter Kali Willows, multi-published author, former social worker (like me,) graphic designer, creative spirit, and newly a publicist. She was perfect, and she and I instantly meshed. We quickly constructed a plan to make this book set sail. We planned a book launch and a book tour. She was a lifesaver when it came to creating handouts, posters,

365 Days Single

redesigning my website, and navigating how we were going to do this mini book tour. I know broadcast, and she knows publishing. Together, we became an unstoppable team.

Once we mapped it all out, we set out on the journey to promote it over a couple of months leading up to the big book launch on my birthday in the beautiful county. Kali and I shared some good times and even greater laughs on the road. Honestly, my newfound freedom was as refreshing as our road trips from Ottawa to Kingston to Toronto. We hit up book stores and media outlets together and on our road journey, I decided to let her have access to my Tinder account I'd created a week before.

Tinder has to be the fastest way to meet new people, it just requires a quick eye, a good hand to swipe with and a strong mind to drown out the assholes who will no doubt be running game alongside you. I couldn't be bothered swiping all the damn time, so I joined Tinder Gold, which is probably the laziest way to date. Once you pay a monthly fee, you can change your location even if you are not presently in that location, which I think is amazing if you were thinking about moving and explore your prospects.

The best part is that anyone who swipes right (that affirms he likes you) gets put into a folder you can view at any time. You can check them all out and swipe the ones you like or leave them in that folder forever, if you please. I signed up for a six-month membership before I went to bed, set my settings to out of town, and woke up to over six hundred men in my folder of guys. I had to do a double take.

Now, not all guys were good looking, I assure you, but it sure gave me an idea as to what is available in the dating world these days. I was blown away at the selection and began checking the whole world out. Miami, LA and New York, because they seemed like the hot spots for men. It was like a smorgasbord of sexiness in Paris, though. Who wouldn't travel to Paris? It's a real eye opener, ladies, to see what is truly out there from the comfort of your own home. Romance-challenged people should sign up and look around.

Tinder was a source for entertainment for my publicist Kali and, as we drove the many, many kilometres between here and there, she swiped left and right. Having someone else's perspective on who looks or sounds good is always a good thing when you have so many bad choices on your own. I thought, why not? She has been married for twenty three years to the love of her life, and I trust and value her opinions. It's actually not a bad idea to let someone else navigate your dating life based on how they see you and what they think would work best for you.

At this point, I had opened myself to a new point of view and to learning more about how the world sees me and how I see myself. Over the rest of the summer leading up to the event, I dated some of her choices. To be fair, they were no better than the ones I picked for myself. With so much going on, I found I wasn't as into dating as I thought I'd be. Other priorities began to hold my interests. I was window shopping for possibilities but left my "wallet" at home.

The event was on the horizon, and I was bursting with excitement. I had conceptualized an exciting outdoor event at the new boutique hotel in Wellington, Ontario called Cribs on the Creek owned by local Michael Hymus. He had just finished off his two properties and wanted to showcase their full potential as an event venue. I laid out the entire concept, and he was thrilled to take part and back the project.

Two hotel properties merged together by fencing, tents,

365 Days Single

tabletops, a caterer, and a fabulous DJ from Toronto, Mark Kufner. The whole thing was so perfect, it in essence became a red carpet event with all the trimmings. Again, if you aren't excited about celebrating your accomplishments, who will be? It was an incredible feeling to bring my book to fruition and make it a reality. I said I was going to do this, and I did. A lot of my near and dear friends were all around me celebrating this momentous occasion, and relief blanketed me.

The book was out. I'd successfully shared my personal story of my life, loving and laughing along the way. It was all out there, and it felt so good. I then immediately thought, wow, this book is either going to bring the right one to me or I will be un-dateable forever. If anyone reads this book and still wants to date me, then they are the real deal. Oh well, love me or hate me, I am me, and I love myself more now than ever before.

The idea behind my *Unlucky in Love* book was not to gain popularity, but to be honest about my love losses and adventures with the hopes that it would connect with other people who felt the same way. If there's one thing I know, it's that there are a ton of people who feel the same way. Love is the thing that drives us with the need to obtain it or drives us crazy. Once you have it, you feel untouchable, and when it leaves you, it leaves you broken. Love is such a powerful emotion, and we all have difficulties with it at one time or another. In my case, more times than not. Things are changing, though. I can feel it deep inside. Something is shifting in the atmosphere as I batten down the hatches for the rest of the ride this year. It's undoubtedly going to be a bumpy one.

As soon as this book launch was wrapped up, I began to work nervously on the second book. It was already in production, but now it was full steam ahead and by full steam ahead, I mean writing daily, dating, researching, and discovering what would be truly best for me. I still don't know what that is.

At this stage in the game, if you are on your own journey, you may still be just as in the dark as I am. I could say I know what I don't want, but that doesn't even resonate with me anymore. See, I have never had a problem finding love or having men love me. I just could never feel the true reciprocation of it for any extended period of time or at all. The game plan at this point is to keep my head up, my heart wrapped up, and my focus inward. To love myself and my own company has always been easy. Whether or not I can allow someone to love me and for me to love them back that has proven to be my Achilles Heel.

Lesson: When you plan to stay single for a year, summer will be your enemy. You need to have a plan of action in place like I did. Mine was focusing on myself. I planned things to do with friends. Focus on my launch for my first book. I caught up with friends I'd promised to catch up with forever. One by one. Week by week. Getting through summer being single for a serial monogamist is the equivalent to finishing the Boston Marathon for a competitive athlete. You naturally want to win. In this case, I wanted to win myself back. That is all. The struggle is real my friends. The struggle is real.

Never Run into a Burning Building

When you navigate through the emotional landmines of the dating world, you really need to consider the hidden dangers. Some of them aren't as hidden as we fool ourselves into thinking. Those dangers are people I call "burning buildings." People on a crisis or angst-driven mission to escape the pain they've walked away from, but the burns continue to sear beneath their emotional flesh. Not everyone who is separated or in the midst of a nasty breakup is a "burning building," but in my earlier days, I had a tendency to rush in and attempt to rescue them.

These are the people facing a painful moment. When things have fallen completely apart in a relationship, they run screaming out of it. Just like you would a burning building. If you see someone running out of a burning building, would you run into it? Heroes do. People like the idea of being a hero. The prospect of helping others feels like a positive endeavour, doesn't it? A deep-rooted need in my past always led me to be the hero in my relationships.

If this type of dynamic is what makes you tick and gives you a sense of purpose when connecting with others, all the power to you. However, make sure that being a hero isn't going to take anything away from you that you can't do without. This is where I've been burned, many times.

The balancing act of giving and receiving. Not many people can afford to give of themselves if they won't receive anything in return. As I grow and learn, I've shifted my thinking this way: someone who is leaving a bad relationship is in a deficit of love. If they weren't already lacking in this area, why would they be leaving?

Ask yourself this. How have you felt in the past when this has happened to you? My guess is, you were hungry for love. Maybe so famished you would grab anything that you could find to get your emotional nutrients.

Depending on the length of time will drive how badly you want to fill up all the empty spaces with a newer supply of it. Most people can't help it. We are genetically engineered on an emotional and biological level to need, to connect, and to have companionship. Humans aren't designed to survive alone. It starves our souls without that sustenance we crave.

When you meet someone fresh out of a relationship, tread carefully. Most men in that situation exist in a state of panic. They can't help themselves and I think for the most part, psychologically, instinctively, it's not their fault. In my dating history, men have offered me the sun, the moon, and the stars and told me anything and everything they thought I wanted to hear.

I've learned not to believe everything I hear anymore, because if they truly mean what they say or promise, their actions will speak louder than words. Those actions need to consistently take place over a period of time. Anyone can text you endless messages and send emojis of unwavering adoration. Someone who wants to spend time with you will make the time and create the opportunities to get to know you.

Your personal values need to be strong and sure in order not to get lost when voyaging through the dating world. If you don't up your value, no one else will, either. Other people's estimation of your worth is unimportant. You need to start treating yourself like you're a Mercedes, even if you think you're not. Don't settle for being a bus pass or a skateboard. You're a human being with needs, you aren't just put on this earth to meet everyone else's and be left unsatisfied.

If you don't set a value on who you are as a person, no one else will. It's taken me forever to really embrace this philosophy. I've always valued who I am as a person, and I have known what I have to offer, but you don't want the car sitting on the lot forever, now, do you? Of course not. Every once in a while someone will take you for a test that is called a date. You'll learn about them. The more dates you have, the more you learn. Hence, when someone is running out of a burning building, you don't let them run into your house and set every valuable thing you own on fire. A guy who has been scorned or neglected in a marriage is on a faster mission to even the score than any woman looking for a husband for the first time.

This analogy brings me to a guy who caught my attention. He was an early swipe for me on Tinder and I admit, I got sucked in fast given his incredible good looks. Like many people, I've had some Hollywood crushes that still resonate with me when I notice potential connections. TV undoubtedly has shaped my view of a virile man. It started with *Magnum P.I.* because who can resist a sexy moustache and a Ferrari to boot. Tom Selleck had it going on, and it seemed I liked cops from way back because I also had a crush on Erik Estrada from *CHIPS*.

This new Tinder guy was a combination of Erik Estrada and Doug Gilmour from the Toronto Maple Leafs. Neither of which I had a chance with, but I had the next best thing, a broken man who looked like them both. The visual appeal draws you in, giving you a sense of those long-time crushes coming to fruition. Lookalikes are the next best thing, right? He professed that his wife had strayed and hurt him so badly that he came running in this direction faster than you could say Usain Bolt.

    This burning building spread his fire faster than Wi-Fi. He was on a mission and within a week, he was in my city unexpectedly on a Friday. My friends and I already had plans to attend some concerts that weekend. His eagerness and the opportunity led me to give him a try. This was his first real weekend out as a single guy, so to speak, and I thought why not go for a night on the town and have some fun?

    Typically, I would be head over heels for a guy who made such a huge effort. He drove down the night before, stayed in a hotel, and texted me at work to tell me he was a little groggy from driving overnight and trying to find a hotel in the city when so many had converged for the concerts. Not knowing the area, he'd ended up in a trashy hotel.

    In the past, I would have taken this as a sign of how badly he wanted to see me, but this time, I reminded myself it was his need to quench the pain of being cheated on that drove him. At least, that's what I believe. I know the feeling all too well. I kept the need to avoid getting emotionally involved at the front of my mind as I made an effort to explore this connection. I took this mini weekend overhaul project on with both hands and even obliged his request to arrange for a small makeover. What was different from my prior need to quench someone's pain was this would be a platonic interaction and nothing more.

    After a haircut and some freshening up, I helped him to pick out new cologne. Why not, right? Retail therapy works for women; a new style and some updated clothes and we're back at the starting line. Over the course of the weekend, we went out for dinner, visited several wineries, and wrapped it all up by snuggling.

This was a conscious decision and one I was proud of. I knew where he was at emotionally… still on fire. He had run from the burning building, and I knew he would regret sleeping with someone outside of his marriage. I didn't want to be anyone's regret, so after an innocent weekend spent enjoying city life, we parted smiling as I sent him back with well wishes and a good luck.

Progress, I was making progress!

A year later, I checked in with him and asked how he was, what happened with his marriage and did it all work out. He was happy to share that after his wife strayed, she realized she had a great husband. They stuck it out and worked on their relationship, which he reported was now better than ever. On some level, I suspect his efforts to reach out to someone as a retaliation for betrayal was the wakeup call she needed to see her marriage was in danger. Sometimes we need a kick in the ass to realize how lucky we are. He obviously loved her enough to overlook her indiscretion. If we ever cross paths again, it will be in the most pleasant way, and if he is with his significant other even more so. I don't fault anyone for following their path, and I am happy I was able to give him a lift without burning my own house down.

Once again, progress.

Lesson: Dodging the "burning building" will require skill, and it will take a few attempts to differentiate a full-on blaze happening from a diminishing flame or a smolder. Just remember, like I made of point of doing, you're not a firefighter— speaking—and trying to save someone from their situation will take a huge amount of energy. Keeping with the thought that I wanted to stay single for a year, this burning building was not going to be extinguished by me.

365 Days Single

Good luck if you come across the same. Leaving someone in a situation that is less than favourable seems like a heartless and inhumane thing to do. You can't save anyone right now is what I told myself. I have to save myself first, so stop, drop, and roll on outta there!

Go With the Flow but Know Where You Go

Early on, when I vowed to be single for a year and date with my eyes open, I realized I was going to have to learn to go with the flow. Jumping into a relationship with someone as I typically do would be my ongoing challenge and a hard habit to break. I can honestly report this has been the most uncomfortable journey of my life. I've had to make continual, conscious choices to force myself to do the opposite of what I've been conditioned to do.

At first I found the process confusing. As the old adage goes, if it feels good do it. Sometimes the "feel good meter" is broken in us, and we mistake what's comfortable for enjoyable. Comfortable is the idea of what we know, the norm, something familiar, and our habits direct our decision making process. Most of us don't associate change with feel good. As much as we want excitement, the idea of change is often scary and not something in our best interest. At least, not until after we've survived the first attempt, or maybe the second, or tenth.

Going with the flow sounds so easy. People say it all the time to each other like it is as easy as breathing. It's not for me. Many of us are hardwired to take control of the factors that determine our lives: jobs, relationships, everyday choices that move us toward something. For those of us who have suffered trauma, this need to control and stick to what we know tends to become engrained in us. We become hypervigilant about anything and everything around us, sometimes to the point where people can perceive us as critical or nitpicking. The reality is, when unresolved trauma rules your inner

365 Days Single

workings, we become conditioned to control the environmental factors within our control so we feel stronger and less vulnerable.

We want to go where we want to go. If you got into your car in the morning to go to work and your car took you in the opposite direction and dropped you off in the middle of nowhere, I guarantee it would unnerve you, if not totally piss you off. That's not where you planned to go. That's not where you wanted to be, yet, there you are. A different location, late for work, looking for a ride and trying to backtrack to where you first started.

That's a lot like what happens when we get into relationships. We get into them expecting to move in a particular direction. When it doesn't go that way, we get mad, frustrated, and sad that things fell apart. We need to understand the balance of seeking and exploring possibilities without adding timelines and pressure points to ourselves to land the perfect mate without further investigation.

If you get into a situation with someone too quickly and have no idea if they can truly navigate the path you want to go, then you're at their mercy. Maybe they lack the competency to get you there, or maybe they don't even know where the hell they're going. It could be even worse—they could be just hitching a ride in your life, hoping you know where to go. This doesn't work, not for you and certainly not for them. Who wants to spend months or even years heading in the opposite directions?

To give all of your trust they are the right driver for your ride, you have to be able to assess if they indeed can take the relationship in the direction you hope for. When car shopping, we don't buy just any vehicle without checking what's under the hood. If we invest in a car, we put a lot of thought into how well suited it is for our needs, don't we? Does it have all the features you like? Good gas mileage, comfortable seats, a solid warranty if something goes wrong? It's a necessary convenience, and you depend on it, just like a relationship. So shouldn't we all put a lot of thought into choosing potential partners for a relationship?

It required being patient and breathing. Not rushing into a situation for the sake of being with someone or wanting to please them and make them happy. You need to make yourself happy first. So the practice of going with the flow was really made so easy by meeting a person I'll call Eff.

In between my Tinder explorations, I still met the odd person organically. Organically is what I refer to when you meet someone outside of social apps, the good old-fashioned way. In fact, the moment I met Eff, the door was wide open and we were surrounded by hundreds of people. I couldn't believe that nobody else saw this Nordic beauty. He was perfect from his softened lips, and chiseled jaw to his golden mane of hair and impressive athletic frame. I love European men. Not only are most European men more mature, I find they have a certain mystique to them others don't seem to hold. Something about eccentricity is alluring.

We bumped into each other in the midst of a crowd. I took my time in learning more about him. He seemed shy, which, I learned later, he actually wasn't. Mindful not to give the impression I was overly interested, I was relaxed in our interactions. Never show your cards to anyone, ladies. It may not be the best thinking, but dating is like a game of chess. You need to calculate your moves if you're going to play and win. I think every woman should try and play above the league she think she is in and stack her odds.

Don't take a shot at just one and expect to get a bullseye. A person firing a machine gun has a better chance at hitting a target

365 Days Single

because there are more bullets. Shoot with more bullets in your dating gun and you will have more success. Don't get hung up on one particular person, until you learn everything you need to know about them. It takes time. Don't commit right away because first impressions wow you. If you rush too quickly into dating someone new that you think is a perfect fit, you run a greater risk of getting hurt. For now, you should be learning to go with the flow and take it slow. There is no rush when you have no immediate destination. Which I don't. I keep reminding myself that this process is going to take time.

The new goal is to not have a relationship, and this guy taught me that every time. Eff was non-engaging and wasn't all over me and messaging me even if I asked him to. Before my new approach, I would've been upset if someone wasn't pouring their time into what I was doing or liking my latest post.

Eff was different, and change was good. I learned from him to take it back a step and give less of myself upfront, too. I used to be like him when I was younger, carefree, and in no rush to be someone's spouse or long term love, which is why I never got married till I was forty…and we know how that ended up. Like an Alanis Morrissett song – "Ironic." You have nothing to lose by waiting, playing the field, and just letting things be as they may.

Ensuring I limited the amount of time we spent together helped me reach my goal. No cuddling or major intimacy kept things a hell of a lot cooler. It felt strange at first, but it did get easier. I saw Eff casually, and as sexy as I found him to be, I knew we would never be more than casual acquaintances, and I was okay with that. Dating someone from another country is an added risk in romance anyway, because you never know when they might go back to their homeland. We're still friends and always will be.

I learned a lot about my friendship with him and I admire his being a gypsy of sorts with an emotional coolness. We could all adapt that a little and maybe protect ourselves a bit more. The fact he didn't actively pursue an emotional or physical connection encouraged me to be a cooler and calmer version of myself. Instead of looking for similarities between us, I just accepted who he was and enjoyed his company. Eff had zero plans outside of his work, and with that I knew that he wasn't looking to make plans with me either and that was a great feeling. We are always so fixated on making plans. Meeting people with expectations of what we think each person is going to bring us because we feel time is working against us. Dating without expectation is probably the simplest and best advice I can offer from my journey. Time is going to go on with or without our approval or control, so we should slow down our dating train and learn to go with the flow. Breathe in and breathe out and enjoy the ride.

Beware of the Cupcakes

Cupcakes are one of my favorite things in the world. A variety of cake flavors and icings are available, and they seem so innocent in small doses. Just cute little confectionery delights that can be reduced down in caloric size so you don't feel too bad about eating one. So much yummy goodness in a couple of bites.

Cupcakes are also really hot and buff guys, at least if you adhere to one of my best friends' analogies. I nearly burst out laughing the first time she referred to a buff guy she was seeing as a cupcake. A cupcake? I listened to her explanation, and her analogy was much the same as my take on the baked good. She likes both kinds of cupcakes, though and if you like dense cake, then you should love both. I, however, have never have been much of a cupcake lover outside of the bakery delights. It can happen to you though, at the most inauspicious time. Just like passing by a bakery window and you see the sugary goodness through the window. The confectionary goods are so tantalizing you can almost taste the sugar on your lips. Just like when you meet a buff-and-fluff guy, which was my first cupcake on Tinder.

This man was a good-looking Middle Eastern guy, we will call Igo. Igo came on super strong with his sugary sweet-talking messages. Note: sweet talking that consists of sweetie, babe, honey, or anything that is usually reserved for more intimate relationships is a serious red flag. Cupcake alert!

Cupcakes are so very tempting and admittedly, I have gone there a time or two before. As a rule, it usually doesn't last long.

365 Days Single

They're pretty and charming, and most likely dipping into more than one batch of frosting... You got to watch those cupcakes, ladies. Too much sweetness will rot your teeth and mess with your pancreas. If a man calls you sweet names all the time and typically doesn't use your given name, it might beg the question of how many ladies he's sugaring up at a time. Have you ever seen the movie *John Tucker Must Die*? The girls described this player behaviour perfectly and it resonated with me. If they use these sweet names, they lessen the risk of saying the wrong name...food for thought, or cupcakes for many.

This guy caught me off guard because he wanted to Facetime right away. This approach seemed overly eager because most guys like to hide away behind social media and the Internet. Not Igo. We chatted quickly. He wanted to meet, and I suggested a date, then he said he wasn't really someone who made plans too far in advance. Why I wondered?

I told him, "Okay, you don't like to make plans. Cool." Delete.

If he wanted to date me he would find me on media somewhere else. If you can't look at your schedule and pick a date, then you are not the guy for me. A day later, when he saw I'd deleted him, he added me on Instagram.

Igo: *Why did you delete me? I'm jealous now. That means others are talking to you now. I'm hurt.*

Out of courtesy, I offered a little insight because I knew I couldn't be the only one who would have been put off by his behaviour.

Me: *I deleted you because I don't understand the point of communicating if you can't or are unwilling to make plans.*

That tune changed his approach, and suddenly he inundated me with photos of houses he'd built and photos of his life and worked to convince me that I was wrong to delete him. I had this odd feeling I had met this person before. In fact, I had, or rather a number of variations of him, men I refer to as "Gatherers." They like to gather women, compliments, kisses, and whatever else can fill them. My first take was run, just delete and block, but I had committed to exploring things in a different way, and so for the sake of learning, I decided to try. Maybe he was a different man in person. Maybe his online attempts were a result of awkward urgency.

As it turns out, very much like I suspected, he was like a true Casanova, and I will explain why. I arranged to stay at my girlfriend's house on the night of our date, because I resided out of the city and did not want to put myself in a situation where I had to stay and compromise my intentions. Which were solely to check this guy out.

Me: *Okay, we can make a date and talk in person.*

Igo: *What fragrance do you like, and I'll wear it all the time. My favourite is One Million, it's been a scent for years now. But you would also love Tom Ford, but I won't take a chance tomorrow and stick to my original scent.*

Me: *Don't change anything on my account.*

Igo: *I have brand new sheets as well, just in case you decide to stay over.*

Me: *Thank you, but I won't be staying over. We're just meeting.*

Igo: *I'm just putting it out there. You don't have to stay over. I want you to know that's how I am., I say what I mean. And so you know, there's no food here, so I'll have to buy some for the morning.*

Me: *To be clear, I said I won't stay over. We are just meeting.*

365 Days Single

It was a pleasant surprise to find from the moment I met him at his condo until the end of the date, he was 100 percent a romantic. We took an Uber to this beautiful Parisian-themed restaurant in the Distillery District. I love Paris! So, it totally was a hit with me.

Over dinner, he was charming, sweet, open, and talkative, and there was a moment when I looked across from him and felt I was looking right in the mirror of who I used to in my twenties. The conversation was so lovely, and the bartender and server complimented us on how nice we looked as a couple and wanted to know how long we had been together.

Of course, when we confessed this was our first date and that we met on Tinder, their eyes lit up with shock and delight. How could two pick each other out so easily and get on so well? It must be sheer luck. No, I don't think so. In hindsight, I think maybe I picked him because on a subconscious level he reminded me of parts of myself, but those parts were long since gone.

For that matter, so was Casanova by the time we got back to his place and he realized that I wasn't going to stay overnight, despite all of the trouble that he went to. I left after we had agreed to meet for brunch the next day. Even when I was driving back to my girlfriend's house, he messaged me and said if I was too tired to drive to her house—twenty minutes away—that the offer still stood to come back and crash.

Me: *No thank you, but good night.*

The next day, as promised, I arrived at his condo to take him for an early brunch. To my surprise, things dramatically changed from his sugary sweet persona. I had suddenly been placed in the "friend zone."

Let me explain how this transpired. I arrived in his condo and asked to use the bathroom right away. I'd had a large coffee on the way. I gathered he didn't expect I'd need to use the restroom and had probably forgotten about what I'd find in there. He went out to the balcony deck to wait for me. In Cupcake's toilet, floated a tiny cigarette with lipstick on it. Hmm, I thought. I left last night around 10:30 p.m., and twelve hours later, here was this cigarette in the toilet. I took a breath, walked past his open bedroom, where I noticed a messy bed. I then went out to the balcony and sat down and smiled at him.

"So," I asked, "whose cigarette is in the toilet?" Smoothly, he offered he had a friend in the building who was having problems with her boyfriend last night and came up to speak to him. Fair enough, I thought, if that is the truth, he's a supportive friend.

I was committed to seeing brunch through, so we left, and my other girlfriend joined us to eat and do a little shopping after. By late afternoon, in the friend zone was where I remained, which was fine by me. I dropped him off at his condo, and we said our brief goodbyes. I texted him one last time and that was it.

Most cupcakes require way too much attention, time, and ego stroking for my liking. Just like Igo. All that constant adoring and approving can distract a girl from her life and her own goals. I wasn't about to fall into that trap and get caught up in the needs of someone else and neglect my own. I needed all the time and attention I could give myself if I was going to make it to the year's end. It's all about my own self-discovery this time around. It's not like egomaniac cupcakes would notice you not around anyway, because they have so many other women chasing them.

Maybe you know one cupcake who isn't dense like the cake version, who is buff with more than fluff between his ears. Then he's not a true cupcake! Because "cupcakes" are just that, dense, fluff on the top, and you only need one to satisfy you. If the physical gratification is the only thing you want, then maybe he would satisfy you. It's different if women are the "Gatherers," though. Don't let the cupcake know you have anyone else on the side or, worse, another cupcake. They can't handle you having more than one cupcake at a time. Their ego can't deal with it, nor would it make sense to them, since they are so perfect in their own minds. Igo wanted a harem of women to adore him, and there was no way I would ever be able to satisfy his giant ego, and so I moved on at warp speed.

Lesson: The careful and delicate balance for me was wanting a strong and confident guy who could be in sync with my own self-confidence but wasn't overly macho or egotistical. I had gathered by now that I needed a guy who was soft and vulnerable on the inside and not afraid to be that because he was strong and confident. I could always find one or the other, and I was attracted to both. Too much of one or the other bored me .and I realized I needed the balanced combination in a single person. It's a tall order, I know, but I wasn't in a rush, so for once, I continued to wait it out.

Stacking the Deck

Okay, I'll be brutally honest. Dating sucks. There are some great times, but there are also a field of potential landmines that can sway even the most devoted believer in love. This chapter is my attempt to stack the deck and build up possibilities, but some were serious duds. If you're currently venturing out into the dating world, you may be really, painfully aware of what I'm talking about here.

All right. I'm anchored, avoiding cupcakes, and I feel like I am still headed in the right direction. I've spent so much of my life focused on one person at a time. That's the old school way of thinking and doesn't apply to modern dating. Too much time is wasted doing something one-on-one, and unless you are in high school, you have no time to waste.

Knowing what works for you and what doesn't is really important when you are dating. Most people try to compromise and adjust to accommodate someone else, because that's the most natural thing to do. It is engrained in us to do so, especially in women. It is what it is. I know I've spent my time adjusting to someone else's needs and schedules versus sticking to what really works for me. I never wanted to be the bad guy. I never wanted to be labelled the selfish person who didn't bend. That has always been looked at as a redeeming trait by others, flexibility. People always give accolades to you if you are accommodating. It's like a gold star in being a good human, yet, I feel, more times than not, with this approach, you compromise so much of yourself that you don't know who you are anymore and are just bending over to make someone else happy.

That can't happen all the time. I wanted to live with intent and get to know what truly is good for me and what isn't. I've never trusted men. That is a huge statement to make on my part and probably a crushing one to hear by anyone who ever dated me. The truth is, my trust was broken so early that I learned the only person you can trust is yourself. After so many years of dating, I lost faith that the next person would be the right one, and my old feelings of fear always resurfaced, convincing me they would betray me. Every. Single. Time. I've thought I dated with an open mind and with the concept that what will be will be. I always felt a chemical connection meant that there was something more happening. I never understood why the hell things were not working out the way I had hoped. My Oma used to say, in her thick German accent, "Don't put all your chickens in your basket." She never understood English metaphors.

I would say, "You mean eggs, Oma."

"Eggs, chicken, it's all the same."

This experiment in open dating without expectation was going to give me a very clear picture of who works for me, what my old habits were, and, if I stuck to it, hopefully show me how to break them. If you are dating more than one person at a time, you are going to see very quickly, in a small scope, what you like and don't like in romantic potentials. You're also going to meet similar types of people you've dated in the past and realize in a snap that they didn't work for you before, so they won't work now. It took me half my life to get to this place where I could see how my tumultuous, damaging childhood laid the foundation for continuously picking the wrong guys and running from the good ones. Overcoming my fear of anyone being too emotionally close had been a long and arduous journey. At the very least, I wanted to be clear on who was worthy of my trust and who really wasn't. So begins this Dating 411/911.

ALEJANDRO

An exotic beauty who spoke Spanish with such a scintillating accent. He had a beautiful story and a lovely soul, but we would have no future other than being friends. At this point in my calendar year of hard lessons, being friends was all I could handle anyway. What he did teach me, though, was there are incredibly sweet and wonderful young men out there. The kind who would drive an hour and half to bring me food when I was sick, do my dishes, and sleep on the couch, just to make sure I am okay. There are romantics out there who would check in on me and drop a message to brighten my day with no expectation other than to make me smile. Consistently being a gentleman even if it meant it was only as friends. There are good guys out there, who've had difficulties and struggled to get where they are, yet are not jaded by their experiences. Ones who always remained true to who they are, unaffected by the bullshit. I admired him and his tenacity for living. Alejandro reminded me to look forward, move on and believe that love was out there and that it would find me.

CARSON THE DAD

Mr. Come on Strong is the key factor for Carson. On the plus side, at first, he liked to talk on the phone and wasn't a fan of texting all the time. He met me for a drink one time at Yorkdale Mall, and I sensed there was something odd about him. He sent me the same photo of his kids at a dojo on two different occasions. I found it

365 Days Single

weird he used the same photo to describe where he was. My Spidey senses kicked in, and, if you know me at all, you know I go with my gut instinct. It may seem small to another woman, but deep down, my lie detector lit up. I don't sway from my train of thought. If I ever believe a man is lying and he can't convince me otherwise, I will cut all contact and ties. I don't have time to hear explanations for what I see as a blatant lie.

Me: *I don't have time to talk on the phone often.*

Carson: *Call me if you're interested. Please don't text me again, I would prefer to hear a live voice. Sorry, I'm old school that way.*

CARSON THE COP

Yeah, back to the cop thing. I've been there, done that, I even wrote a book about it. Well, a chapter anyway, and said I would never again date any officer of the law or anyone in the legal world. Not because everyone is exactly the same, but at some point you need to declare a moratorium on certain types of guys. I don't even think it would have mattered what his profession was. It was his personality and the way he operated that turned me off.

The back-and-forth messages and then convincing me to make plans with him on his off days and cancelling the day of. He rarely ever liked to talk on the phone and only texted. This man wanted to "sext" with me, which I'm not a fan of. Especially if you're at the beginning of getting to know someone. Don't sext with someone you barely know, and be cautious of who you do that with if you ever do send naughty messages. The cyber world is scary, and bad things can happen if the wrong people access your private words or photos. The fact that someone who works as an officer would carry on like this shows poor character. It was a no brainer for me, I was done almost instantly.

Carson*: Would you consider spending time with a guy in Toronto? I like the sound of that. I'm off for a few weeks. I'm very attracted to you. I like your energy.*

Me*: I would prefer to meet in my hometown and not in Toronto, since I don't know you.*

Carson*: I think that's a great idea, I would love to see you.*

Me: *Cool. How's Friday?*

Carson: *Cool.*

Shortly after this exchange, the sexting inundated my phone...delete. This was supposed to make me swoon? What the hell happened to chivalry?

BRETT

This man made the effort to be sweet, charming, and persuasive in text and then totally dropped the ball. Brett made plans with me, then cancelled them. He tried to explain and then said he would call me back. Sure, life can get in the way. It happens to everyone. Deep down, that lie detector beeped again. I figured he had a better offer come up and if that was the case, he could have just said plans changed, and I can't make it. Don't lie. I've been in the dating world long enough to recognize a lie. If you can't make it for whatever reason, that's perfectly fine, but have the decency and basic consideration to call and cancel. Texting to cancel plans is disrespectful. Period. If someone texts you to cancel plans, the likelihood they'll show any deeper consideration toward you in future planning is slim to none. One small thing can grow into bigger things. He tried to reconnect a few times, but I just don't go

365 Days Single

against my inner voice, especially when it screams at the top of its lungs. Sorry.

Brett: *Ok, I'll say you're attractive.*

Me: *Thank you, but looks aren't everything.*

Brett: *Well, let's be honest. Looks are what catch us first, creating our desires, and getting to know each other is the fun part.*

Me: *There's no harm in talking.*

Brett: *I'm not like anything you've described you don't like, and I'm aware you're in high demand.*

Me: *... (Speechless).*

Brett: *What are you doing now?*

Me: *I'm just getting ready to head out.*

Brett: *That's the most erotic thing ever. I'd like to watch you get ready...the buildup as I sit there dressed up and watch you lather, apply, moisturize, strut, and prance as you model your choices...*

Me: *...wow (speechless again.)*

Delete. How can this be considered courting? Have we diminished ourselves so much through technology and interactions that women you don't even know are simply fantasy fulfillers over text messages? How is that supposed to work for us? It's supposed to be dating, not solicitation. Yeah, baby, tell me more...delete, delete, delete.

TREVOR

This mysterious person was a former athlete who would send multiple messages of adoration and then disappear for a period of time. This routine continued for the entire year and even though he only lives across the border, we still never saw each other. We would chat, then he would disappear for a few months and resurface with messages. The last time we reconnected, he said he'd been dating some girl and it didn't work out so he reached out to check my status. Trevor wanted to make plans. We chatted a few more times, and I still didn't see him. He was hot as hell, but I was never sure what he was searching for, especially because he sent me photos of bondage items he purchased online. That in itself didn't bother me. Whatever floats your boat, I thought. The likelihood that his boat was going to float over here from the USA was pretty unlikely. If he ever does, I hope he brings me shoes.

STEVE

Steve is an ex-military man I communicated with for a short time. Despite being so sweet, kind and charming with his every word when we spoke, the fallout over a week of talking to this guy was super ridiculous. How can you be so together and then completely do a 180 in behaviour and attitude? He said he was suffering from PTSD, and I could relate to a lot of what he expressed he felt when we spoke.

It was frustrating to see it in someone else and knowing that he was far, far from discovering who he was, so I cut my ties with him. The fact that he was a smoker was a huge no as well. Optimal health and wellness is part of my lifestyle. I work to keep my body healthy, and this journey is to improve my mind and spiritual well-being. Steve was sweet, but he was in the wrong head space to even consider exploring further.

ETHAN

365 Days Single

At the beginning, Ethan struck me as a possibility I was willing to explore over time. He came across as sweet, articulate and was a striving entrepreneur. He was handsome and could be quite charming—at first.

There are a few red flags that people need to be aware of when dating, and they may be so subtle that you overlook them at the start. If you live with your brother and you're in your forties, that's fine. There's no shame in shared living. If you do have accommodations like this and wish to pursue dating women who have an established life, please make sure you have adult furniture. Ensure your place doesn't look like a college dorm or bachelor pad for twenty-somethings who have no direction. I'm not a petty person. I've been on my own since I was a teen, and I work hard to make a life for myself. I take pride in my home, whether it's solo or with someone. If I wanted a twenty-something, I'd date one.

Ethan didn't own a pair of scissors, a wine-bottle opener, or ice-cube trays. He kept his box spring and mattress on the floor with no bedframe, a situation I'd expect from adolescents who've recently moved away from home and are struggling to make minimum wage. That's understandable. It takes time to build up and establish yourself, but for a man in his forties, it's a huge red flag. At some point of adulthood, one typically develops a lifestyle or aspires to it. Plastic containers and drawers are for storage and are not intended to double as furniture.

As for assessing potential stability when you're dating someone, if you're interested in someone who loses his job within a few weeks of knowing you, or doesn't own his own car, you might want to ask yourself what the circumstances around this are. Have they led you to believe they're more settled and established than what you're actually finding?

If you look past these little things because, as we know, we've all had our own run of bad luck, all the power to you. Maybe there's a diamond in the rough going through a transformation. Great! If you're motivated, you can get past it.

If this same guy takes you out for dinner and gives dirty looks and speaks sharply to anyone who looks at you, then you made need to wake up and smell the dysfunction. If this same person who is showing more insecurity as you spend time together then begins to accuse you on another occasion of paying attention to another man simply because you can't place their face and glance at them a few times to jar your memory, you may just be in dating hell. Especially, when the person you are trying to place in your memory is over sixty years old and you're sitting at a public table with two other women and having a nice chat. The fact that I'm a public figure and know literally hundreds of people in my community wasn't going to improve this person's insecurities. It added layers of dark, encompassing jealousy that indicated any future public appearances would lead to more of the same.

To think I was totally into this person initially when he swooned me with their words. I was head over heels for the way he worked to get my attention by being constant with texts and phone calls. That faded quickly after a few dates when he showed me his jealous and insecure ways. I never had the heart to tell him what I saw in him that would just not jive with me. It was much easier to take the fall for why the dates would not turn into something more. Too much was said too quickly, and his insecurity would never work in my life. I've dealt with that before, and I'll never go back to it. No sense in talking about these things with someone who may not see their jealous and insecure ways. No one wants to hear that about themselves, and I didn't know him long enough to delve into this with him.

NIKOLAS

You know when you find a perfect guy who has everything going for him and you think, this is it, this is what I've been searching for. But then, you start to feel there's something missing between the two of you. It's frustrating. You wonder, how can this be? Handsome, intelligent, and athletic, with a killer smile. He owned a home, drove a nice car and came from a great family. He was there for his ailing parents, had strong family ties, and was a gentleman in every way.

Disciplined in his fitness regime, he ate healthful meals and made me dinner a few times to showcase his culinary skills. He'd also worked his way to the top in his profession. This guy was flawless, and we really jived together in conversation. However, deep, genuine chemistry is something that just resonates between two people so naturally and you can't make that happen no matter how hard you try. Sadly, with Nikolas, it just fizzled.

I'd gotten to the point by now, there was so much going on at once. In between all of those guys I got to know, there were even more who I simply talked with to learn more about. I explored the different personalities and what I was attracted to. I kept my eyes open and got to know different people to see who I actually liked. There is an old saying I like, "Variety is the spice of life." It really is.

The more you get to know the variety, the more you get to know who you are through their eyes and through their demeanor. So much of what I learned from the guys I actually took the time to get to know better reflected so many of the previous guys I dated. I would be in mid-conversation or sitting across a dinner table from them and realize I'd been here and dated this type of person before.

The scope of men gave me a clear and precise vision of what would work and what wouldn't. Now, all I had to do was wait and see what would develop with this new knowledge. I was impressed that I had made it past the halfway point and still had no boyfriend and had stayed true to dating, being single, and not falling back into my pattern of serial monogamy.

Lesson: The hardest part so far is to date without a long-term intention. That was the flack I got from random people who thought I should just be celibate for the year and avoid contact with men. Celibacy was never something I signed up for. Yes, I became a lot more selective about who I shared my personal time with, but I also stuck to my guns about not jumping into sexual relationships that would muddle my focus and create confusion about my self-discovery. I need to be able to walk in this world in a new way and be able to handle meeting people, getting to know them, and not engaging in a relationship. I needed to be comfortable letting people down before they got too attached if they were not a suitable fit. This was the most difficult thing to achieve, because nobody wants to hurt someone's feelings. At least I didn't. It sucks to hurt someone, but I have been hurting myself the most for the longest by not letting them go sooner. Hence, being a serial monogamist for so long. Just rolling from one to the next because I didn't want to hurt

365 Days Single

anyone and had no idea what was right for me anyway.

The Halfway Checkpoint

It's now more than halfway through my year and it has been a struggle, but I'm hanging on. The past six months have been the most difficult, but the most pivotal, because clarity is beginning to happen. I love my life. I'm growing to love who I am. I'm strong, independent, and I've proven that to myself. I feel it in my bones. I can breathe freely, and no one can take that from me.

I won't compromise myself and allow someone to be more to me than I am to myself. I will be present—in the moment and not live in fear. It happens only in baby steps though. I can't run into love before I walk. I know with certainty I'm on my own two feet. I've dated and enjoyed meeting different people and allowing myself to say no when it doesn't feel right, when it's not a good fit. I will never again get involved with someone because I can make them feel good and make their lives better. After redefining my purpose, I'm comfortable with the idea of feeling good about my new ventures and have no regrets moving forward.

Yes, I still want to find love. Like the quote from the movie *Practical Magic* where Sandra Bullock writes, "I dream of a love that even time will lie down and be still for."

Unlike my rushed attempts, I now know I want to fall in love slowly, like slipping into a warm bath. With someone who truly wants to be with me, who will hold my hand as I step into the warmth of a genuine, long-lasting connection? That person who will ease my reservations and support me as I transition and surrender my entire self for once. The one who will stand by my side as I allow the emotion to embrace me without my old fear of being hurt taking control of my heart anymore. The person who, for the first time, will help me remain present and stay grounded in the relationship I so deeply crave.

    I know I can't dive into the sheets with someone that I want to be with because that's going to confuse how I feel, just as it always has. In an attempt to better understand how I fell for this time and again, I came across a handful of articles that explain the science behind the euphoric feeling after achieving an orgasm. They all suggest it's a biochemical response. After the throes of passion take us to that blinding moment of release, the brain plays a trick on women. It sends oxytocin into our blood stream, otherwise known as the "love hormone," which promotes the sense of bonding.

    In a nutshell, this means she's more likely to fall in love with the person she slept with, especially if it's a particularly satisfying moment. The downfall to this physiological marvel, is that most men will do and say anything to get you into bed. Sure, they may feel the same euphoria at the time, but men seem designed to shake it off easier after the fact than we do. It seems unfair the universe would stack the cards against us so. We get pleasured, bonded, and then left in the dust while the guy gets his jollies and, in many cases, moves on to the next toe-curling rendezvous. Women are often left with lingering feelings from having shared this special moment with someone, and then make the soul-crushing discovery that it didn't mean the same to the other person. Ladies and gentlemen, this is what breaks our confidence in finding love. Opposing sides react differently. Don't get me wrong. I know the tables can be turned in cases where women seek out the physical release and men are left holding the emotional baggage. I'm just relating from personal experience.

If you succumb to physical intimacy, then you may have just put the odds against yourself. Resist at all costs if you're really looking for love. That way you don't run the risk of getting fooled by smooth talkers and brain chemistry. Pretty easy, right? For a die-hard romantic, it is the most difficult thing to do.

Here's a solution that can help reduce temptation—look after yourself first. That's what vibrators are for, girls. That should be your major purchase if you're single. Ideally, to remove any possible confusion, you should consider taking care of your own physical needs, and take the edge off before you go out on a date. I'm not suggesting this to be crass. Keep your mind and body in check or you may be leaving yourself wide open for hurt. Old habits are hard to change for anyone, but if you want to bring Mr. Right into your life, don't be Miss Right Now...unless that is all you want from them.

Love sets you up to succeed, but only if you know the rules of the game. I hate to refer to it as a game of love, but it is and we all know it. Be smart. In suggesting this, I imagine you won't listen to a woman like me, with an unlucky track record. I never listened to anyone's advice, either. It wasn't until this past year, at forty-six years of age that my brain and body start co-existing and listening to one another.

You can't make someone love you, even with sex. Using sex to find love backfires. Why on earth does it have to be so damn difficult anyway? Why are there so many apps out there and online dating sites to help us do what should come so naturally? Because it is not easy. So, stop beating yourself up every time a date or relationship ends. You need to remove expectation from you and your potential love interest and what you think each other should be doing. We

365 Days Single

can't control our own dating destiny as much as we'd like to think we can, but you can protect your heart a bit more in the process of allowing someone to get to know you. I'm not saying to shut yourself down, but tread lightly and don't throw it all out there at once.

Mistaking attraction, passion, and lust for anything other than what it is, is a dangerous game to play with your own emotions. Logic and heart are really not designed to co-exist. The heart hungers for what it wants. Experts say you can't control who you fall in love with. I believe what we can do is slow down the process by not sleeping with someone right away. Make it last long enough to give yourself some mental clarity. Which is what I've implemented at this point.

The person I was long ago had no interest in taking things slow, but that was before my world got turned upside down. Little did I know the greatest love of all was going to leave me soon. I would be unprepared for what was going to happen in my world, but I feel like the minor change I made helped prepare me for it unknowingly.

Meditation. I began the practice of starting my mornings with five minutes of quiet mindfulness, after I made a cup of coffee of course. I gradually worked my way up to ten minutes of quietness before I headed out to my radio job in the wee hours. Ten minutes was all I could spare, and I only did it consistently on weekdays. However, if you add all the minutes up by the time the year ends, it's more than it would have been if I had waited for twenty to thirty minutes to free up in my day. I made the most of it, and I kept going with the flow.

LESSON: Dating while being more mindful and more connected to who I truly am inside. The process of the daily

Orlena Cain

meditation and just clearing my thoughts every morning helped me significantly. I think the lucid moments in the morning, just as I awoke, was the time I could hear my own true thoughts before the noise of the day set in and all the worries and doubts started talking to me.

The Greatest Love of All Leaves Me

A defining moment came in the fall of 2017. One that would change how I viewed love and what it truly meant. I thought I had experienced true love when I was young and in my twenties. Karlof, who I discussed in the first book, was one of my sweetest memories, but I have had a few other brushes with what I thought was love since then. My greatest love met me forty-six years ago on the day I was born. Not my biological mother, who never loved me or wanted me.

My true love was the one who did not allow my mother to abort me or adopt me out. My true love, being my beautiful Oma. She wanted me to stay in the family and loved me from the very beginning of my life to the very end of hers. The love that grew between my Oma and I over time was so genuine, so pure, and so true. She always made me feel so special. I was the sparkle in her eye, and she was the sparkle in mine. I am so blessed to still have a wonderful Auntie-Ma, my Oma's daughter, to love and care for me as Oma always has.

These two women were instrumental in making me feel like I mattered in the world and was worth fighting for. After all, they went up against my mother many times trying to save me from the terrible abuse they knew I faced daily. So much so, that Oma and Auntie-Ma escalated the situation to protect me. They tried to pick me up from school and ended up having restraining orders placed against them. That was one tactic the Villain forced my mother do to get to me. If it wasn't for Oma and Auntie-Ma's combined forces, I may have had nothing to live for. Knowing I was worth something to someone gave me hope and purpose.

As a little girl, I would lie awake at night and think of escaping the house of horrors. This house was not a home. It was a place of despair and loneliness. Thinking of leaving was unfathomable. There was only one time in fact that I was ever brave enough to leave. I was maybe about eleven or twelve years old. My cousin Robert had come to visit for the day. It was a very rare occasion for me to be allowed to have anyone over to the house, so having him visit was a treat. We had talked that day while he visited, and I told him, without revealing too much, how awful it was at the house, and he told me I should run away. I'd never even considered running away before. This house, as awful as it was, was all I knew. I had grown accustomed to the pain because it was an everyday thing that no one in the house ever tried to stop. As cold as my mother was, I didn't want to leave her and later, when my little sister was born, I'd felt I had to stay for her too. I was burning out and thought maybe I should run away with what energy I still had. Robert left that afternoon to go and stay with our Oma for the night, and his suggestion seeped into my subconscious and soon, my dreams.

The next day, in the still of a beautiful summer's morning, I slid out of my single mattress on the floor of the tiny hallway where I slept. I trembled inside, but I felt the confidence from my cousin's words of encouragement to run away. The worst things had already happened, so I figured I had nothing to lose. I grabbed a piece of paper and a pen, wrote a note, and left it on my bed. Avoiding the creaky spots on the stairs, I crept quietly down them, opened the back door, and snuck out to the garage. Slowly I opened the garage door, glancing up at the back window that overlooked the backyard and farm. I kept wondering, is anyone looking out here? Can someone see me? I grabbed my bike, closed the door, and walked it to the driveway slowly. If anyone did see me at this point, I could just say I was going for a bike ride. But where should I run away to?

Oma's house! She would take me in and protect me. I jumped on that bike with the fierceness and force of Lance Armstrong. That hill was the Tour de France, to me, and I was going to pedal up it at lightning speed. Bursting with fear and courage, I only glanced over my shoulder once to see if anyone was looking out the kitchen window. I made it to the top in seconds and down the other side of the hill. I estimated that it would take me about a half an hour to get to Oma's house if I kept this speed up, maybe less if I pushed hard. I pedaled so hard and as the air whipped through my long curls, I smiled into the sun. For a moment, I felt free!

I arrived at Oma's house and ran in like I was on fire. My Oma came out of the kitchen with a shocked look on her face, but my cousin Robert just smiled at me because he knew why I was there.

"I did it. I did it," I shouted. "I ran away!" My Oma asked where if my mother where I was. I said, "No, and please don't tell anyone I am here." She didn't have to, though, because the phone rang and my mother was on the other end asking about me. It wasn't long though before she showed up to take me back. I begged her to let me stay at Oma's. I didn't want to go. I feared I'd be beaten with even more force for my disobedience.

Leaving, I burst into tears. My mother was the worst person in the world next to the Villain. This woman was his silent accomplice, just as bad, doing his bidding. I was quiet and couldn't look at her the whole ride back. My mother never asked me why I ran away because she knew. In case anyone didn't, I'd outlined it in my letter.

I am running away, because I am tired of the beatings.

Simple. I was also tired of being molested, but I hadn't added that. We arrived back at the house where the villain and his mother waited for us. To them, I was the crazy one because I'd found the spark of inner courage to rise up against the abuse. Ever so slowly, I was rising.

Oma was one of those special ladies. The power of her convictions runs through my veins, and the way she faced the trials early in her life have always given me the courage to be strong, to hold on, and to push on.

Born in 1927, in Heidelberg, Germany, Bertha Elizabeth Posmick was just twelve years old when World War II started and eighteen years old when it ended. She had experienced her share of heartache and pain seeing that up close. The greatest of atrocities to mankind surrounded her on a daily basis living in Germany. She arrived in Canada as a young woman and cooked to make a living. She was beautiful. Her porcelain skin, curled hair, svelte figure, and humorous spirit made her instantly likeable. Her nickname was Betty, and it suited her gregarious nature.

Betty was a force to be reckoned with through her whole life. She raised five children, worked full time and co-existed with an alcoholic and abusive husband. She was kind and loving, but firm, like an iron fist in a velvet glove. I spent my first four years mostly with my Oma in the farmhouse she'd raised her children in. I also bounced around from time to time with my aunts, Susan and Donna—Auntie-Ma.

My mother was around, but never wanted me and we never really bonded as mother and child should, so it was the love from my Oma that made me feel happy to be in the world. She loved me so much. I was her little girl. I feel my mother resented her for making her keep a baby she didn't want. My biological father came around from time to time to see me until I was four, but my Oma's love surrounded me always.

That pure, unconditional love stayed with me on my darkest of days. Her love was always just a phone call away. No matter where I was, I could always call her and she was there every single time to tell me she cared, she understood, to love me when I didn't love myself, and to always know what to say to make it all better. My soul felt so connected to her. When I look back at pictures of her and me, I can see a love between us and something about the way she looked when she smiled in the photos was visible in my expression, too. I felt this woman's love deep within me, and through the years we grew such a special bond. We shared so many moments that made me feel this way.

When I was a little girl, living on the farm, and no one was allowed to visit me or take me anywhere, she would take the heat for showing up unannounced at the house all the time. Occasionally, she would be allowed to take me to church, and after mass, we would go to McDonald's. It was freedom in my eyes, but I would never cry to her or tell her of my sadness at home. I didn't want to waste our moments together with sadness. I was so joyful to have her in front of me that I would just smile and feel the love from her radiating across the table. I remember seeing her car come up over the massive hill on my darkest of days, her little brown Comet would be like a ray of sunshine. Whenever I saw her coming, I would drop what I was doing and run to the driveway, overjoyed to have someone who loved me show her presence.

Each time I saw her, she'd wrap her arms around me, and I

365 Days Single

would throw my tiny arms around her legs. She seemed so tall, but she really was no taller than I am now at about five foot four and a half.

I've felt this love within me even when she was far away and I would think about her every day. Every single day, I thought about her and carried with me the lessons she taught me through her words and her actions, the tolerance she showed to a husband who never deserved her, patience and hope for things to change with an abusive alcoholic man.

Oma's never-ending strength was incredible. Always forgiving and hopeful. More than I imagined I'd be capable of. That hope and forgiveness for her husband ran out more than ten years ago when she became too ill to care for herself and could no longer be his caretaker and servant. My Oma and could not navigate around an old farmhouse anymore. So when he refused to sell the farm and move to a smaller, one-level bungalow, she prepared to divorce him. After more than fifty years of marriage, she'd finally had enough. That's a long time to wait to divorce, but for many of her generation, when you married, you stayed with it, regardless of how hard it was. She had no choice left and after many falls she had to leave.

Her husband, my grandfather, was and is a stubborn and selfish man. He wouldn't even buy a coffee for her if he was standing right beside her when she ordered it. His sins are lengthy, and I will not speak of them, but I lost all love and respect for him when I was sixteen years old and saw him punch my grandmother in the mouth and knock her dentures out. It was a traumatic experience. In that moment, I grabbed my Oma and put her in the car. I begged her to leave him.

The separation forced my grandfather to sell the farm and give her half of everything he had although he lost the most valuable thing he had, her. If he'd recognized that, he would have treated her like the queen she was. My Oma enjoyed more than ten joyful years after she left him. She stayed with family initially and then moved into a retirement home. I loved to see her be taken care of for a change. Her health steadily declined over those ten years, though. I would visit her often and sit and just have tea with her. I would bring her favourite sugar-free candies and treats and enjoy her companionship.

When I most needed that comfort and love of her all around me, I'd stay over with her and sleep beside her, just as I did when I was a little girl. We would cuddle and she would speak the words I needed to hear. Those were the best talks. All those words she shared with me when I was sad, scared, or worried.

In the fall of 2017, my Oma fell sick and had to go into the hospital. Her visits there had become frequent as her body began to break down. This time, it felt different. I prayed she would improve and return to her home quickly. After a day of tests, though, the doctor told the family only a complicated operation might save her. Without it, she would die, but she also stood a chance of dying in surgery. Her age was a big factor. The doctor wanted to know what the family's wishes were.

My heart ached. I knew what was coming, and I wasn't prepared for it. I visited her in the hospital every day. I stayed by her side for hours. Other family members close to her were there as well. The decision was made to make her comfortable so she didn't suffer. She was in and out of consciousness and steadily slipping away. Her last week here on this planet was an agonizing one for me. The love of my life, who put the sparkle in my eye just as much as I put it in hers, was fading away from me.

Her last day here on this earth was a beautiful one for me and symbolized my love I had for her. I had a book signing for my first book that took me away from her for the day and I rushed to get back for that night. My publicist Kali travelled with me that day to support me, because I was so out of it and scared Oma would leave me before I could get back. I could have cancelled the book signing, but I knew Oma would have wanted me to celebrate my success and fulfill this commitment. So I went, and I prayed. When I returned, I grabbed my pj's and headed to the hospital to see my sweet queen and sleep beside her. I had no idea this would be the last night she would be here, or did I? Was that bond between our hearts so strong that I knew?

Perhaps. All I wanted to do was not leave her side. The staff at the hospital brought a bed so that I would be able to lie close to her. I held her hand confessed my love for her before falling asleep with her hand in mine. In the morning, she was still with us. My heart was filled with bittersweet joy to be beside her, even though I knew the end was coming. It was a divine privilege to spend these final hours with her, and I drank up every last second I could of her presence. The doctor had told us it would be any day.

Oma had a steady stream of visitors in her final hours. Family and friends who came to say their goodbyes and pay their respects to a remarkable woman who had impacted so many lives for the better. I came by for tea with my uncle and relieved him so he could grab dinner and come back. I just wanted to sit with her. Once he left, I held her hand once again and whispered to her how she was the best grandmother I could have ever had and that I loved her so much.

This private moment was my confession of my love for her. Her eyes were closed, the monitor was beeping and in her deep unconsciousness she heard me. I know she heard me, because she drew in a gasping breath and slowly whispered, 'I love you too." I smiled and kissed her softly on her forehead. My uncle came back in the room and I left to go home and he said he would call me if there was any changes. I told Oma, "I am going home, but I will be back, okay?" I kissed her a final time and left.

When I arrived at home, I poured myself a very stiff drink and returned some calls. While on the phone, I saw my uncle's number come up and my heart sank. I answered, and he said, "She's gone." I was in shock even though I knew it was coming. I dropped the call and grabbed my shoes. I paced in the elevator as it dragged down to the bottom. I ran to my car and sped to the hospital just minutes away. I ran from the parking lot into the hospital so fast that once inside while I was pacing to get in the elevator, someone asked if I was all right. I said nothing, because at that moment, for the first time, I truly felt nothing inside. All I could think of was getting to her, my Oma.

Inside the elevator I braced myself for what was waiting on the floor above. I would have to face the finale of a beautiful life and a good bye that I never wanted to have with the purest love I'd ever known. When the doors opened to her floor, I felt her presence still and ran down the hall way to her. My uncle and his girlfriend were there with her, and I collapsed at the side of her bed and took her hand in mine. She lay so peaceful and so still, and the imminence of her departure was before me. I held her hand gently and felt it cooling. I kissed her face and nuzzled in her neck to smell her skin. I did this over and over again, telling her how much I loved her, and an explosion of tears soaked my face and rolled down. I could feel my heart fracturing like glass.

She was really gone. Her body remained there, still and peaceful, but she had left me. Devastation flooded me, and I dropped to my knees crying, gasping for breath as my Auntie-Ma and uncle arrived. Unable to move a muscle, I just stayed on my knees, crying, because the acceptance of the end was more than I could bear. My chest was so heavy with grief, I could hardly breathe, and the true depth of my sadness hadn't even surfaced yet. This woman loved me like no other, and there would be no more hugs, no more kisses, no more tea for two, no more visits or road trips. No more memories shared. This would be the final memory of her physical presence.

That day in the fall of 2017 my heart shattered into a million pieces and its fragments dispersed through my entire consciousness. I didn't want to leave this room with her in it, ever, but she was gone. I had to leave. I didn't want to see the orderly take her away from me. I wanted to leave on my own.

A good friend of mine, Erick, who'd recently lost his mother, showed up at the hospital to help walk me back to my car. Every step was agonizing as I trudged away from her for the last time. I had to take breaks along the way to gather myself. The journey that had taken moments before was so long. No one can prepare you to lose that kind of love. Grief crashed over me, and the emptiness consumed me like nothing I'd ever felt before.

Lesson: After living all of my days with my heart filled with so much love from my Oma, it was terrifying to face the days ahead without her there anymore. Yes, I had her memory, but I didn't have her touch, her hug, her warm smile and kind eyes to look at me anymore. No more words of wisdom in any future moments of despair. Now, I had to rely on my memory of who she was to me. I had to face the world without her, and I felt stripped of every sense of protection I had ever carried. I had become truly vulnerable for the first time. This devastating loss seeped into the deepest regions of my soul. The flooding of the dark, cold emptiness jolted my mind into a new reality. This would be the beginning of a new life. One without her. The only way to face it was to be courageous and strong, just as she always taught me to be. In these moments of loss, we can only remember what was and pray for the strength to continue.

Clipped Wings

You can only imagine what happened next after losing my Oma. A crushing monsoon of indescribable sadness, heartache, and shock swept over me. It felt unreal, like living in a dream. A roller coaster of emotions was on the horizon for me and in more ways than one. The day after we lost my Oma, I was asked by my aunt and uncle to clean out and pack up her room at the retirement home. When I passed through the lounge, some of the residents asked where Betty was and I whispered, "She passed." I walked along the hallway as I had done many times before and rode the elevator for the last time, two floors up.

At the open door of my Oma's room, I stood and stared. It was so empty now. Not just due to her lack of physical presence, but also in the way that her energy usually filled a room with warmth. It was a cold, sterile room with no comfort to be held in her absence. She wasn't coming back to lay down or have tea in her chair with me. That realization clutched my chest like a vise grip. I took the boxes and bags inside and fell to her bed face-down as I inhaled the remains of her soft scent. I wept and grasped the blankets to my face, as I broke down, yet again.

In a bid to lessen my devastation, I put some music on and opened up her drawers and closet to sort and pack away all her possessions. This was it. Her entire existence in one room. Her ninety years compartmentalized in such a small space. It hurt so badly, but it had to be done.

My saving grace to push through this hardship was the arrival

365 Days Single

of one of my best friends, Laura-Lee. I'm so blessed to have her love and support. We wept together, hugged, and periodically remembered funny stories about Oma as we sorted the final pieces of her existence. Knowing me so well and the state I'd be in, she also brought some wine because that's what good friends do. They bring wine and help you through the worst possible moments.

Laura-Lee and I have been through some amazing things together, and we've been through some real shit, too. Here she was again, helping me with one of the most difficult things I have ever had to do. She helped me pack it all into my car, and I selected some of my favourite Oma clothes to put in my front seat of my car. I was in a complete haze at this point. Probably still in shock from everything that had just happened. I really had no idea what was going on at all in my head and probably should have just headed home, but I wasn't ready to face any of the real world yet.

How have you coped after losing someone so precious? I wanted to run away. Far, far away from my grief. With my Oma's clothes and belongings in my car, I drove west. A guy who had reached out to me, Rick, asked me to go with him to an amusement park that day. This may seem like a bizarre invitation, and I sincerely didn't want to go, but a brief escape to push away the pain of loss for a few precious hours held an appeal.

My head was spinning, my skin felt tight, and I wanted to burst and scream out to the universe with rage and sorrow. Being on a roller coaster actually proved to be a cathartic release. I wanted to scream at the top of my lungs, *"Come back to me! I love you!"*

The drive on the highway was quick and when I arrived at the park, Rick was happy to see me. I was so disoriented that I can't recall a single word he said. He offered a carefree distraction to help avoid my feelings, and he offered it with no strings or expectations. I just wanted to go on ride after ride and scream endlessly until I could physically expel the sadness and the gut-wrenching pain.

When tears would form in the corners of my eyes, I would wipe them. People probably thought I was crying from the ride. Maybe the wind was too much for my eyes. I spent about four hours there before I couldn't take anymore. I felt disoriented and sick to my stomach, my sadness quickly morphed into rage, and I wanted to punch anyone in my way from the park to the exit. I had to leave and face the inevitable truth that my one true love had left me and was not coming back.

The drive back from Toronto was long, although getting there had seemed short. The gentle scent from Oma's belongings filled my car and swam over me. I grabbed one of her shirts and wrapped it around my neck and breathed her in on the way home. The wisps of her filled my nose and her memory enveloped my body. She'd been gone a full day, and I was dying inside.

I took a week off from work and spent it letting the grief fill me and spill out into oceans of tears. I cried when I awoke and when I went to bed. My heart had completely broken. It was then I realized how deep her love and this loss impacted me. No man I'd ever dated ever impacted me on the same level. Sure I had heartbreak, but had developed a knack for curing the heartbreak of one man with another. I couldn't do that this time. I couldn't replace this emptiness with anyone else.

Oma was someone truly special and irreplaceable. During this time of sadness, Rick tried to insert himself into my life. This was never going to be. We crossed paths at the worst possible time, and at that point, nobody was going to get past my steel walls that had

365 Days Single

built themselves up overnight. Once there had been a three foot fence, maybe, as a deterrent, but no moat, or drawbridge had ever been so quickly erected. The steel door had been locked shut with an army of emotions to guard it from being brought down.

As I look back, I feel bad for Rick, but I don't know where this guy got in his head that I wasn't able to fathom the concept of dating, let alone anything like that when the love of my life had died. My heart was in pieces, and I didn't want anyone to touch it or be near it. I didn't want comfort or consoling from anyone. I didn't want the pain to go away. She was worth every salty tear I could cry. So, that's where I was.

Right after I dated the perfect guy, I met the perfectly crazy guy. The most unattractive thing to someone is an overeager dater. Someone so desperate for a connection they can't let you breathe for a second. For a few weeks, I was met with a barrage of text messages from Rick that started out sweet and nice and then quickly escalated to adoration.

It wasn't coming from a bad place at all, I just didn't want anyone around me at this time, and the more he pressed, the angrier I got. I had to be mean to get the contact to stop. In a tailspin of emotions, I couldn't relate to anyone or let them into my world. I needed to mourn and process this tremendous loss and void. I felt naked every day I stepped out of my condo and felt so empty inside that. Some days, it made me really angry to feel so vulnerable. Such strange emotions were coming over me, and I did my best to make sense of it all without hurting anyone. The best thing I could do was make my way through my day and get home so I could cry alone. There was no room in my heart for anyone, and my future looked bleak. In case I haven't made it clear, this part of my journey was probably the easiest time to stick to staying single.

Lesson: When you feel despair and sadness, nobody can tell you how to navigate through it. Grief is a personal thing, and it is immeasurable. You, and only you, will know how to deal with it. It affects us all differently, and the best thing you can do is be prepared for the worst feelings to consume you and pray you have the strength to make it through. Lean on those who love you, and don't push people away. Some days, I just wanted to have coffee with a friend and not talk about Oma at all. Other days, she was all I could talk about. You go through it as you feel you need to. Love is such a precious thing, and the loss of it is devastating.

Moth to a Butterfly

Winter was fast upon us, and it's the one season that no one wants to face alone. Yet here I was, still grieving, and it was just weeks away. I had become slightly numb without my Oma, but I knew I had to somehow try to reassemble my life without her. What would she want me to do? Now that she was on the "other side," I felt she could see everything that I did, and the last thing in the world I would have wanted would be to disappoint her with how low I sank into my grief.

So much of what my Oma had told me was so true. She never thought I would have children, and even though I entertained the idea with a few special connections, I never did move forward and have my own. After my marriage ended, she said she didn't think I would ever get married again. Were those her visions of no marriage or children a reflection of what she would never wish for herself? As I progressed after that heartbreak, it turned out I didn't actually want to get married again. It wasn't until after she passed that I realized I had grown to feel this way.

I wanted to have my own family, though, even if it was just a family of two. Being in your forties gives you fewer options of having a relationship with someone who has no children. I'm not against children. It's the drama from the history attached to ex-wives or girlfriends that comes along with it that I choose to sidestep altogether. I've had good situations and really bad ones. Unfortunately, it's the really bad situations that leaves a bad taste in my mouth.

365 Days Single

One ex-wife was so mean she absolutely dissolved the happiness in my life, simply by being so bitter about her own divorce and her own choices she made, which had nothing to do with me. If their ex picks up the pieces and is happier without them, the egocentric ones can't stand to see someone else happy. These vengeful, bitter people will go to great lengths to make all those around them miserable. It's toxic. I never want to have to deal with that again. I couldn't comprehend the concept of territorial jealousy when it comes to children. If someone else is really good to your children and loves them, is that not a good thing?

Even though I never had any of my own, I would expect if your child survives a marital or family split, the more love they are surrounded by, the better. Especially if those new partners respect the mother-child bond and never try to interfere with it. In some cases I've experienced, the jilted women were so insecure about being replaced that they subjected their children to even greater damage by stressing them out over who they allowed to love them.

During this fragile time, I realized I needed to shield myself even more and kept my guard up more than ever. Of course, this was the precise time something twisted happened to test my strength. Why? Why when I felt my defenses at their lowest would someone try to squeeze their way into my life with their future wishes?

John came into my peripheral through a simple swipe. I never once considered him to be someone who would be an appropriate choice as a potential partner. Again, I'm keeping myself open to explore possibilities and better understand myself. He was so determined that he went to great lengths to sway me with his charming words. Mere words mean nothing to me anymore. Actions speak louder than words. Actions determine that value you place on someone.

Time is valuable and you can cut and paste any message you like to ten people at once. I know, because I've done this myself in the past. Everyone responds differently to the same words based on their feelings about you. It's eye opening to say the same thing to different people and see their response. Very eye opening. I wouldn't encourage doing this with anyone that you are genuinely interested in, but it is a good experiment just to prove how a well-typed text can influence people. I've been swayed in the past with written promises of commitment and caring.

These days, I'm less apt to believe someone is serious about me based on just what they say, and even less so by what they text. It has to be a good combination of the two. If you haven't learned this through dating yet, you may be stuck in a rut, where you keep doing the same things over and over again. If this is the case in your situation, it may be time to pause and consider making adjustments. Take a breath. Look at what you've been doing. Has it worked for you? If not, it might be time to try doing the opposite. That's what I did.

John had an angle, but it didn't matter what he said in text because his actions revealed the polar opposite of his carefully crafted words. My feelings never were hurt, because I took what he said with a grain of salt. It didn't matter what fancy or enticing lines he cooked up, they fell like a deflated soufflé in the end.

Growth is a painful thing. You place yourself in a cocoon to protect yourself during a time when you feel most vulnerable. I felt more so than ever, and my energy was depleting at high-speed. I had always kept busy. Goal setting was my way of getting far enough from things that have hurt me. I knew by setting goals that even if I

365 Days Single

failed, I'd still have a positive focus, and if I achieved my goal, I'd feel fulfilled inside. As it was, I'd already accomplished so much that I was proud of. I'd stumbled along the way, and made a ton of mistakes and bad choices, but everything has led me here. I firmly believe in the saying, "Everything is as it should be." I knew now what I had to do.

My whole world shifted when my Oma passed. The way I had viewed the world had transformed. I was on a hunt to empower and energize myself from the inside out. I debated different strategies to be able to do all of this and still be true to who I believed myself to be. I was in a phase of rebuilding my strength and needed to make some changes in what no longer worked. I evaluated my friendships, my career, my home, my business, my health and finances. Everything was put under a microscope, and I began to see things so much clearer. Once again, the universe sent me a few more challenges to see if I was ready to grow and evolve, or revert back to my old ways and get the same results.

For once, I had grown tired of the illusion of love and realized all the reasons why most people want love are the exact reasons I never really wanted it, not deep down. I had blindly followed along with what I thought I was supposed to want. Simply because everyone in the world made a huge deal about having love in your life and all the wonderful things it was supposed to do for you. None of which it did for me. I felt love suffocated me, drained me, deceived me, and instilled fear within me.

Having a child was one of those things that went along with the embellished notion of true love. In our twenties, it was the goal to avoid getting pregnant and then in our thirties it seemed society has that pressure on us all to find "the one" and make a family together.

I loved my twenties and have no apologies for them. There were no real expectations beyond succeeding in my career, and I loved that. The difficulty was in my thirties, I still didn't want to get pregnant. Because this was something that defined my approach to life, it was pure torture having to always explain why I felt the way I did about having a family. Despite my honesty, I still managed to get sucked into relationships with men who wanted to try and change my mind. A few times, I was almost persuaded, but the reality would kick in of how I truly felt and I would bolt, leaving most bewildered by my actions. John rehashed all of this in a slew of assertive texts.

John: *Imagine how beautiful our children would be?*

Me: *I'm not sure how to respond to that.*

John: *LOL. You'd better snatch me up so no one else does.*

Me: *I'm not looking to start a family, just getting to know you at the moment.*

John: *Stop running from love, family, and happiness!*

Me: *I'm not running from anything. Having children is not my priority at this point.*

John: *Why not?*

Me: *Several reasons, but my age is a major factor. I'm not keen on being a senior with a kid in college.*

John: *I'll always be around for you and the kid. Hell, I'll be fifty-four when you're sixty.*

Me: *I'm not sure why we're still discussing this.*

John: *You know deep down you've always wanted to be a mommy. You just needed that right person—surprise, it's me! Get to ovulating!*

Me: *I honestly have nothing further to say about this topic.*

John: *Pregnant women are so beautiful.*

365 Days Single

Even though over the years, I've had love interests spout dreams of starting a family, I had never realized this pregnancy thing was an actual fetish until I experienced this particular exchange. So here I was, at the ripe age of forty-six years and provoked to deliberate my choices with a man who I had only been on a few dates with. John had convinced himself that he wanted a baby with me and persisted in talking about it. Keep in mind, we went out a total of three times. He got the idea that I wanted a baby with him not from my lips but from his own crazy idea. This was pure insanity.

Perhaps part of why this provoked me to anger so much was his blatant disregard to having no knowledge of my personal history—one that carried a great deal of childhood trauma. There was no interest in exploring why I didn't want this. For a man to butter a woman up, expecting every woman has a maternal instinct or dying need to procreate...there was a certain irresponsibility in this callous bandwagon he so quickly jumped on. Sure, maybe our kids would be beautiful. He wasn't an unfortunate looking man.

What about getting to know a potential partner before making any major decisions? What about exploring if you mesh as a couple, a plausible team, before you insist on bringing an innocent child who would be dependent on this person to love and protect them into this world. What if that person wasn't capable of that? As someone eager to be a father, wouldn't you want to make sure the person you're propositioning isn't a complete monster? How do you know she'll be a good mother?

Needless to say, my responses ceased and he disappeared back into his fantasy land of big talk and small walk. Maybe this proposition was a player type of angle he adopted to reel women into sex. I certainly wasn't going to fall for it. I'd made a conscious decision not to have children, so his persuasive approach had no impact on me. I hope other women aren't quick to fall for baby making madness as a draw to find true love.

At the closing of the 2017, I really wanted to go into the New Year with a fresh start to my new path. I rarely go out on New Year's Eve, for the very reasons that would unfold on this night. It's never been a great evening for me and with that in mind, I made the decision I wasn't going to drink. My head space was still not ideal. These were my first holidays without her, and they were even harder to navigate than I had dreaded. The glaring intensity of my emotions made me acutely aware of how easily annoyed I could get by people tonight. My prediction was I'd want to go home early tonight and let the partygoers enjoy themselves.

I personally find going out on New Year's Eve the equivalent to having a cavity filled. It's expensive. You can't avoid it. It may hurt you, and it's not always fun. The alternative is to sit at home, but plans change, friends' guilt me, so I go, reluctantly. This encouraged venture was to a plaid and toque party. Picture it. This is where you're going to meet that special someone who can split wood or at least look like he can. For those who haven't experienced this urban wonder, they're called "lumber-sexuals," and I will admit, the beard is goddamn sexy.

If you only look the part and don't actually have any calluses on your hands from chopping wood, then you lose your sex appeal in my opinion. Everyone is supposed to wear plaid and a toque to get into the spirit of things. I don't wear plaid to a party, and I only wear a toque when I'm snowboarding. I just couldn't bring myself to play this game, so I dressed in black. I'm like Johnny Cash standing in a sea of plaid, but with no ring of fire, although when all the excitement of midnight ensued, people were crammed all around the fire pit, and I almost slipped into it. Damn plaid people.

The party proved uneventful, just as I suspected, and to top it off, an ex-lover was there with his new girlfriend. Of course he was. The universe was really messing with me lately. The sad part was there weren't too many places I could go and not bump into one. To have that happen on New Year's Eve just cemented my reasoning for not wanting to go out in the first place. So now it's midnight, and I know from past experience that nothing good comes after midnight. I tell my friends I'm leaving. My friend needed a ride, so I offered to drive her home. She agreed, but once she got outside, she decided she was going elsewhere. I left and headed home. I later found out she fell on the dance floor and sprained her arm really badly. She is a hairstylist. It's not a good choice to stay out past midnight.

So closed the end of the year, and I was looking forward to what the New Year would bring. Little did I know how much was going to change in such a short amount of time of just one year.

Lesson: Sometimes it is good to test your own theories you have about your life. It's healthy to revisit and see if things have changed. The choices I made for myself long ago were still choices that worked, at least when it came to New Year's Eve.

The bigger lesson from this part of my experience, was the eye-opening moment from John. I discovered how even men can get caught up in the ideas of making something from nothing without taking enough time. The brief interaction with him showed me how far I'd come in my journey. It mirrored unhealthy ideas of how to pursue love without having a clue what I was getting into, or the long-term ramifications my actions could cause. My serial monogamy was unhealthy, for sure, but I walked away with the comfort of knowing I wasn't bringing innocent children into a dysfunctional situation to appease my own selfish fantasies. I embraced the new feeling that I had, in fact, grown. I was thankful my stance on becoming a mother remained as it was, true to myself because I know well enough what is good for me.

Into The Light

The beginning of a new year can bring about change if you welcome it. Some people set new goals, change of diet or old habits. Things were about to drastically change, and it had nothing to do with any of those. I never make New Year's resolutions anyway and live the best I can day by day, and making changes when and where I need them. I never leave them till the end of the year. As I said before, the universe hears your words and listens to your quiet thoughts. If your intentions are strong and unclouded, the universe will manifest opportunities to help you move forward and embrace your destiny. I had officially laid to rest any internal conflict about having a baby. I was about to switch gears.

When I returned home an hour after the stroke of midnight, I poured myself a really stiff drink and crashed on the couch. I put my feet up and opened my Tinder account to see what was happening in the world during the hours I had been out. I adjusted my settings to Vancouver to see what was shaking in that part of the country and if there were any better prospects in that vicinity. I loved Vancouver. A few of my girlfriends resided out there, and one I was really close to had always encouraged me to move.

I thought about it, but first, what kind of a life could I build out there? Would there even be any romantic potential to explore? Of course, it's Vancouver, home of the hipsters and lumber-sexuals! As I sipped my cocktail, I scrolled through a stream of guys. Keep in mind, I had the Tinder Gold feature which puts guys who have swiped right on you into a folder. There were a few hundred in there, not all award-winning picks, but I still took the time to look through them. A few guys intrigued me, and one quickly responded. Little did I know that this person was going to be the catalyst I needed to make some drastic changes. I know what you're thinking. Catalyst for change must mean finding love, right? No, my mindset had been transforming, and I embraced something different this time. I came to terms with the fact it was time for changes I needed to make for myself alone. Remember, I'm still learning, but I've evolved in my thinking.

In the wee hours of New Year's morning on my side, and three behind in Vancouver time, Guy, as I'll call him, was at home and had decided to not go out. A pleasant change for a New Year's for me, here we were chatting about almost everything, and I really liked his energy. Guy was refreshing to talk to and full of stories to tell. There was something that seemed a little off about him. I couldn't place my finger on it, but the way we connected felt like I was talking to a good friend.

As we spoke often in the weeks to come, he suggested I consider coming to Vancouver, to meet up and hang out. The idea intrigued me. I'd grown weary of my hometown and the pain that lingered here. A mini vacation might be just what the doctor would order. A lot of our conversation on the phone was very positive, and at times we'd even FaceTime to chat up a storm. He talked a lot about fashion and women, and women who liked him, noticed him, or talked to him. That struck me as odd, and brought me back to that initial feeling of something being a little off. The more I tuned in, it occurred to me he was constantly trying to impress me, which, to be honest, he really didn't. I did want to go to Vancouver for some fresh air and to get some clarity. Not for Guy, but for myself. It was also a chance to see my old friends I dearly missed.

About a month later, I packed a bag, flew out, and met up with Guy. I had my girlfriend Tara pick me up at the airport. Just to be safe, I gave her all my information of where I would be and who I was seeing. Lucky for me she didn't live far from where I was staying. I planned on seeing a few other friends while I was there, too.

The development over the four days of hanging in B.C. made things crystal clear. I strongly believed that he was not playing for my team. I found him to present as a more feminine person. He owned lots of shoes and didn't pursue physical intimacy. When we were in public, he put on his macho game face, which surprised me. He was anything but that. He had a vibe about him that made me feel like he was one of my many guy friends who are gay.

Nonetheless, it was good meeting him, and my trip to Vancouver made me realize things just were not working back home. A change of scenery really can do some good for a soul. That is the good came out of following my path and just moving forward.

When I got back home, I walked through my condo door and looked. My new clarity resulted in the discovery that I no longer wanted to be there. My home had served its purpose. My time of cocooning and hiding was over, and I wanted a fresh new start. That would also involve letting go of the store that I'd built up over the past three years. The two coincided with a place in my life I'd moved past. I needed to let both of them go and the ideas that went along with them. I can't explain where these thoughts came from, but they were at the forefront of my mind. I wanted a new start.

When I moved into my condo two years prior, it was because I was in need of a place to stay. My relationship with the Prince who

365 Days Single

was a Jester came to an end, and I lived for a brief period of time with two very good friends of mine, Jamie and Christopher, before making a decision to have my own place. I'd needed a soft place to land while I figured out my feelings and decided if this move was truly permanent or if I would reconsider and go back. I left the first time for a few weeks, but I felt the move was more permanent if I had my own place. It solidified the end of my relationship and a start of my new journey alone.

In combination with that thought, my store was a labour of love created with the Prince, and it had served its purpose, too. Both represented a time of running from something and toward a new truth. I had no idea that any of this was happening within me during this transition. I'd needed to find myself again, and it had taken at least until the beginning of this book to do so.

As I read back through the chapters of my life and evaluated what happened with those relationships, it struck me that I'd never actually been at a loss for love. I looked back and realized that I had a lot of men who loved me, some I wish I could have loved back, and the rest were giving me a love I didn't want. I didn't just need to cleanse my palate from relationships, I needed to cut loose the anchors of my past so I could freely move forward into something new, healthy, and satisfying. As much as I had enjoyed the fruits of my labour, my store and my condo were now my anchors.

Making radical changes takes an exorbitant of strength which I was running low on from my constantly busy days. Where could I draw the energy from when my daily routine consisted of waking up early for my morning radio show gig, hitting the gym, and then rushing directly to the store to work all day? I was running from 4:00 a.m. to 5:00 p.m. Monday through Friday. A few hours to spare before bed to eat, read, return phone call or maybe relax then bedtime between 8:30 and 9:00 p.m., and I woke up the next day to do it all over again. I had successfully manufactured an extraordinarily busy life to distract myself, and it had backfired on me. I barely saw my friends over the three years that I had the store.

Most of the time, they would come to see me there, have coffee, and catch up with me. Forget about having any time to meet anyone. Even when I did meet someone over this past year, I was so busy, I had time for a date here and there, but could not, nor did I want to, commit to a situation. It was not my time.

So much was turning inside me and I was unsettled. I wanted to be free again, but I needed stability. I needed to fly free again and not be shackled to the four walls of a store. And most definitely not to a store that was created with someone that I once loved. It was time to let it go. The store was my escape, and yet there was nothing I needed to escape from anymore. All my fears had subsided. I didn't know how I was going to go about this. I needed help and little did I know at that time that my mental call to the universe for help would be answered.

Not all calls for help are going to be answered by a knight in shining armour. Sometimes they are answered by friends, family, or by total strangers. When it comes to the inner workings of male and female relationships, I think the go to for most is that when there is compassion and kindness, men and women can sometimes slip sex into the equation based on nature. Maybe it isn't always about a sexual thing between two people.

I thoroughly believe that my Oma sent this person to guide me forward to my new freedom. I couldn't have asked for better timing, and when past meets present, your future can change in such a

365 Days Single

fierce and fast way. When I said I wanted to sell my store, I meant it. When I said I wanted to leave my condo behind and move forward and leave myself open for a new possibility, I meant that, too. I spoke it into the universe and meant it wholeheartedly and I got my answer.

Here is how the chain of events unfolded. I put my desire to sell the store where I knew I could get the broadest response. Through Facebook. I love Facebook. It's a directory to the world, and it connects us to virtually anyone at any time and all at once. In my opinion, it's the greatest invention since the Yellow Pages directory. Most love to hate Facebook, but in moderation, it's a tool that can do so much good. I had a few strangers. Soon enough, an old friend from high school, Debbie, reached out to me.

Debbie had been serving in the Canadian military for the past sixteen years and had even gotten promoted to sergeant. She was an unstoppable force, much like me. She'd raised her daughter on her own as single mom and made an incredible life for herself. I have the best memories of Debbie growing up. I went to my first concert with her in Prince Edward County to see Honeymoon Suite and Haywire, two Canadian bands very popular back in the eighties who were passing through our small area on tour. We were only sixteen years old when we attended the concert, and boy did we have some fun. Truly memorable.

Debbie and I had reconnected a number of years before when she came back to the city. Sometimes she would come to some big parties I threw in the area, and she also stopped into my store occasionally. She loved it and commented one time that she would like something similar one day. Well, that someday came for us sooner than either of us probably thought. She was in the best shape ever while in the military, but that did not stop her from having a heart attack. She never could have prevented it or foreseen it. It's that insidious. She is one tough cookie, and she battled back and survived. However her circumstances were going to have to drastically change. This is where our worlds collided again.

Here we were, two women needing to let go of something that no longer served a purpose and as we let go, we had each other to hold. She bought the store and moved it about an hour away to her city. Which I felt was even better. The Mexican restaurant beside my store expanded. I got my life back, Debbie got a new life, and the restaurant grew in size. Everything just worked out perfectly and in record time.

Prior to the store sale, I had put into motion moving out of my condo. I also decided that I wanted to liquidate some things and store the rest. My time of cocooning was nearing its end, and it was my time to fly like a butterfly into the light of my new life. I wasn't scared, though. This whole shedding the past took shape from my Oma's passing. As I said before, the clarity I got from the change of scenery and flying out to Vancouver made me see things in a different light. I no longer wanted to live alone. So. I sold every piece of furniture that made contact with any guy ever. I only wanted to have my favourite things, and anything that was tangible and could carry energy, I wanted it gone. That is exactly what I did. Everything I put up for sale, sold. The past was officially gone. I wanted a fresh start. I wanted to move into the next chapter without dragging any of my past behind me.

When I started this whole process, I asked a close friend of twenty-seven years if I could move in for a bit till I figured out what I was going to do next. She said absolutely, and my heart finally felt

365 Days Single

at rest. A sense of family, safety, and love, had been restored to my life and I felt relief. Two years prior to this, when I had moved into my condo, she was splitting up with her husband of over twenty years and needed a place to stay every other week till they sorted out their finances. It was my pleasure to help her, and I loved her company. She returned the favour with the same grace, kindness, and love.

I put all of this into motion late in January and then the changes I instilled began to swirl about and take shape. During this process, I met a unique person who was there when I really needed someone. For that I am forever grateful. I connected with this man on such a strong level of friendship. He was thoughtful, hardworking, and handsome. Derek inspired me and encouraged me in every way to make these changes for myself. We had a similar upbringing in a lot of ways and when we first met, it was in my store. A mutual friend introduced us, Derek and we had some great conversations.

These chats made me feel like he understood where I was going on in my life, and he wanted to help me move out of my condo and pack up my store. I couldn't have asked for a better person to come along at this time. He was a good soul, a kind person, and he felt like a really good friend. We spent some time hanging out together over a few months. Derek had a lot of great insight and helped me out in ways that were above my expectation of our connection. I needed a really good friend, and he definitely was that.

The perfect man in a nice, neat package. I felt the need to try and connect with him in a romantic way. At first, it was new, and nice, but after we spent some time together, I began to recognize there was something blocking me from being able to move forward in a way that would make us more than friends. Derek was patient with me and knew enough about my past that he didn't press the issue. I felt awful about it. Derek did nothing but give of his time and energy and helped set me free so I could fly again.

In this process though, I had to admit to myself what I knew deep down. I wasn't ready for commitment yet. Sometimes the connections we make are not for a lifetime, but for a purpose. He helped me through a huge transition. After some soul-searching, I recognized it was time for our connection to come to an end. It made me sad I wasn't able be what he wanted and needed.

Lesson: You should never be sorry for following your own path even if that means you end up hurting someone else in the process. If you aren't being malicious, it's better to end things than drag it on, giving them false hope that you can offer more than you're capable of. That's what's actually cruel. In the past, I would have hurt myself and compromised who I am to be something for someone else, just to avoid hurting them. I spent a lifetime being for others what they wanted, simply to make them happy. That was not me anymore. I had gained the confidence over the year to be me, and for the first time, it felt really good.

Festering Wounds

A journey of self-discovery rarely goes the way you want or expect. In fact, it is best to go into this type of journey with no expectations of yourself or anyone else and simply keep open to what will happen. Know that this will be a challenge; at least it was for me. Staying the course and being dedicated to yourself seem easy, right? I'm here to confess, it's not. Life keeps us so busy with day-to-day responsibilities and events that it bogs us down to a survival mode that makes it hard to focus inward with so much outward noise and distractions. I can promise you, though, from my experience, that the more you stay the course to resolve the issues that have been just rolling off you and tumbling around in your life, the better you will be in the long run.

Imagine when a city overhauls the infrastructure. Let's take, for example, the sewer system, because it is not working the way it used to, and things need to be renewed. The old, rotting structures need to be torn out and replaced with new, improved functioning pieces in order to work. In the time I ran my store in the downtown location, I personally experienced such upheaval personally over the three years. I was kept busy and distracted, but the entire downtown core was torn up. Ironically, now, I chuckle to myself as I think back to it. The answer on how to overhaul myself was happening around me, but I didn't see it or understand the universal message in it.

When you start digging into a foundation and tear out the structure of how the fundamental things of operation have been working, there will undoubtedly be incidents or complications that come up. You can't forecast what will happen in these situations and, just like in your own life when you start digging around in the structure of your past, you will have things come up you are unprepared for.

I may have been rather unprepared, but I welcomed the changes that were beginning to manifest. Once I had my freedom back and the ability to focus solely on me, I made sure I dug deep, and I wasn't afraid of what would come to the surface. For once, I spent time with myself and looked inward. Until then, I never appreciated how deeply I had buried some events and the pain that accompanied them. Despite how open and honest I was with people about these events, I never truly allowed myself to feel and process the actual trauma. In a manner of speaking, I tucked it down deep inside and ran on autopilot as I tried to figure out my place in the world. Like so many people, I had been oblivious to how my childhood was affecting my current way of life.

With so many years between me and those terrible childhood experiences, I saw myself as a survivor. Understandably, I believed that once I got a certain distance away from it, I would be safe. Hence, I continually put goals in front of me and went after them with such force that I knew I would succeed. Not every goal I went after I attained, but I came close to some, and others morphed into a new opportunities. Either way, I was distancing myself from the pain and attempting to layer happiness on top of it.

I liken my path to that of building a house on a cement structure. In theory, it may seem like a solid solution, but over time, if the foundation isn't laid with the proper supports, it's just covering up weak spots. As the weight of the building continues to grow, or the layers, the pressure that builds will eventually start to push down on the structure and that weak spot will cause everything to fracture and buckle in response. Essentially, it turns to quicksand. For so much of my life, I played down what had happened to me in my mind because to actually accept how horrifying it truly was had become far too devastating to cope with. I was a winner, not a loser, and doing myself in would be losing in my mind.

After I wrote my first book, I learned I had been dealing with a fearful-avoidant attachment disorder that people can live their whole life with and never know it. Perpetually going from one relationship to another and simply feeling that each is just not right for you. I would crave love but, as soon as began to feel it, I was terrified. In my case, love reminded me of the people who hurt me in so many unforgiveable ways. It's a very convoluted web of emotions, and I couldn't make sense of my feelings when I became connected to someone intimately. The majority of my early relationships were very short term, and I struggled with letting anyone get close to me. I discovered this after giving my book to a friend who is also a therapist. She helped me learn this through some tests and conversations. That truth was in front of me, written in black and white in psychology books, and I never knew it. But, that was just the start of understanding.

When I began this journey a year ago, I wanted to understand my dating patterns and look at the many reasons I chose certain men and why they never worked out. I met just about every type of guy I have ever dated in this past year. Some I haven't even mentioned because they were brief encounters via a phone call or a few texts. That was all I needed to discover that they weren't right for me. Before, I was the queen of second chances. Always hoping that whoever I was with could be more than I thought or even they thought. I learned this is never the way to go into something with someone. If they don't fit in your life, then you must evict them from it. Simple, quick, and painless…or so I thought.

With some further close conversation in therapy form, and some deep digging on what develops from suffering ten years of horrific abuse, I learned that I had also adapted, but with complex trauma. With this better understanding to aid me, for once, everything about my struggles finally made sense. I understand now that the men I dated triggered me in so many vast ways, and people in general would sometimes bring reactions out of me that were not conducive to relationship development. I lived guarded and always looked over my shoulder because my body responded like the threat had never left.

I had never processed the trauma.

Although I had taken some initiative and engaged in years of therapy with countless therapists, talking about what had happened, it never worked. Predictably, therapy would then evolve into me exploring and talking about my problems in whatever relationship I had going on at that time. None of this really helped for very long. I eventually gave up therapy in my mid-twenties as I felt everything had been resolved as best it could be. With this new understanding about the effect of trauma, I had an entirely different lens under which to examine things.

It wasn't about my individual relationships, it was about the threat the closeness to my partners represented.

Now everything was so clear, and at the same time I thought, "What the hell am I going to do with this information now? How am I going to navigate around this mine field? "Hidden bombs lying dormant in my psyche this whole time, had to be addressed. I had to go back there and walk through this nightmare of emotional baggage. It was necessary to do this in order to find peace. I wasn't afraid to face this new truth because I wasn't alone. I had the love and support of friends around me, some family who encouraged this journey, and I was living with my close friend Laura-Lee who was like family. I was prepared to do this.

My friend Dr. Julie Gowthorpe, RSW, told me about this treatment called Eye Movement Desensitization and Reprocessing (EMDR) that is used on veterans who suffer from Post-traumatic stress disorder. I researched this type of treatment on the Internet, and found statements from a variety of people who proclaimed it saved their lives. I felt I was in need of this saving. I needed to give the next person who loved me a fighting chance, and I needed the same for myself.

EMDR is an integrative psychotherapy approach that has been extensively researched and proven effective for the treatment of trauma. This revolutionary treatment has a set of standardized protocols that incorporate elements from many different treatment approaches.

I arrived at the first session confident and fearless, was excited to clear some of this trauma that had been locked away in my brain for years. During the initial session, we went all the way back to the very first memory I have of being abused. In fact, I was between the ages of four and five, and I can remember moment by moment what happened on that day. In the session, we went back to that day and watched it play back using the techniques of EMDR. Strangely, I felt it wash away, leaving me clear from it. It took over an hour and following the session, I was incredibly tired and immediately went home and slept for three hours.

365 Days Single

My brain needed to heal, and it was the best feeling in the whole world to have it happening. When I awoke from my power nap, it felt like a new day. I was more like myself than I'd ever been. In the days to come, my mood, how I viewed things, and how I saw myself altered. I felt a shift take place within me.

The second time I went in, we tapped into my trauma and pain from the abandonment I felt from my mother and her failure to protect me. I had experienced immeasurable pain from this lack of protection and had isolated myself from her thinking that the pain would resolve with time. I was wrong. Not thinking about her, and sometimes even forgetting she existed, didn't help it go completely away.

What did help was taking time to process it. Using EMDR, the feelings of disappointment, betrayal, anger, hurt, and being unloved were completely resolved. I saw her for what she was and finally accepted it. I made peace with her and understood that she is not me, and I would never be her. Part of my fear was that I would be a horrible mother like her, a woman who abandons one daughter and overcompensates with the other out of guilt and shame. I no longer hold this belief. I have my own way of living, and I would never choose the ways she did. I'm not her, and I'm happy to be free from this ghost in my mind.

I intend to continue on with more of these treatments as needed, to heal my mind so that my heart can be open to the love given to me by another. I see my future as one that allows me to accept love and l genuinely reciprocate unconditional acceptance.

Lesson: Forgotten trauma that was never properly addressed is never truly resolved. It can seep into your subconscious and impact areas of your life in ways you can't see for yourself. Trauma and pain shape the way we see ourselves, the people around us, the world, and our place in it. Early childhood trauma can literally rewire the neuropathways in the brain, leaving a mess of issues to contend with in their wake. When we get to a point where we continue to run into brick walls, we fail at certain aspects of living over and over again, and we need to explore why that is. It's easy to blame situations, circumstances, and even other people's participation in our lives as the precursor to why we can't find happiness.

It's not until we peel back the toxic layers and explore the pain we've spent a lifetime trying to suppress that we can truly understand the impact of the damage. Sooner or later, it resurfaces, whether as fear, anger, or something else, time and again, and can cause more damage with every appearance. I intend to continue with these treatments as needed to heal my mind so my heart can be open to the love given by another and I will be able to feel that in my heart fully and completely for once. I never asked to be abused. I never asked for the people who were supposed to protect me to look the other way. I never asked to be burdened with pain, guilt, and regret. No one asks for those things, but many of us are blindly anchored by it. It's our responsibility to rip the Band-Aids off our festering wounds and disinfect the damage. In some cases, we have to cut out the gangrene in order to survive.

Spreading My Wings

To feel so airy and light in my heart, mind, and body was such a freeing sensation. I could feel myself shifting daily. Little by little, the way in which I viewed myself was changing and when I looked into the mirror, I saw a glimmer in my smile of the young, sweet girl I was before all of the horror started happening. I could see that sweet angel, smiling at me, and normally I would feel this vulnerability and be fearful.

That wasn't how I felt anymore. I saw that and knew I was strong even though I was vulnerable. When I was growing up with the Villain, I was never allowed to show my emotions. My being joyful irritated him, being vulnerable angered him, and my being weak and crying during my beatings was not tolerated. In fact, during my beatings, I was not allowed to cry or show pain. I had to suppress my feelings and hold them all in or suffer an even worse fate. So, now all of my emotions were trickling out of me ever so slowly. My laughter sounded more joyous and I felt alive for the first time in my adult life. I was excited for what was happening, and I felt safe to be me for once. The fact that I was living with one of my best friends, Laura-Lee, an incredible woman who has been by my side for over twenty-seven years was instrumental in my feeling safe to step into the treatment in the first place. Having her love all around me was helping fill the gaps in where it was so empty before, and her home was a safe place. Especially seeing a beautiful, healthy example of a mother raising her daughters, free from abuse.

With the shift happening from the EMDR therapy, I finally

365 Days Single

felt like it was a good time to step further inside myself. I joined a local yoga & Pilates studio called Mindful Movements in my hometown of Belleville, and began the process of really connecting to my body in a mindful and nourishing way. Several of my good friends had been telling me for years that I should be doing yoga and that it would be so therapeutic. I saw it as slow, though, and I felt the people doing it were softies and the vulnerability behind it was too much before. Now, I was ready to be open because I knew I was strong and that nothing could hurt me. Definitely not yoga.

My first yoga class was hatha yoga. Hatha is a general category that includes most yoga styles. It is an old system that includes the practice of asana—yoga postures—and pranayama—breathing exercises—that help bring peace to the mind and body, preparing the body for deeper spiritual practices such as meditation. The studio thermostat was set for 100 plus degree heat, too, so it was pretty intense, but again, I was ready for anything at this point. I stuck to the back of the class, by a window, so I could see what everyone else was doing and could relax and take it all in without feeling self-conscious.

As we moved through the practice, as they call it, the instructor would occasionally say, "Now, let something go." I would breathe in deeply and let my body feel the power of focus, mindfulness, and the strength from within. The yoga class was one of the best classes I have ever taken, for many reasons, and the most important was what happened near the end of class.

I felt I was on the right path, and this moment cemented that feeling in me. I was in a pose that had my body angled to the window and as I took a deep breath, the instructor said, "Now, let something go." At that precise moment, I looked at the sky and a bunch of tiny dandelion puffs floated up. When I was a child, I blew on the dandelion puffs, like many children did, to make a wish, only I would wish to be taken far away. At that moment, I saw a ton of tiny wishes floating to the sky and immediately thought of my Oma. She sent me a ton of wishes to claim, and I let go of a little more of that fear of love I felt, and tears streamed down both cheeks. I wasn't ashamed of my tears and in the 100 plus degree heat, everybody would have just thought it was sweat anyway. So, I never even wiped them away. She was and always will be worth any tear I cry.

I really felt like things were changing. The inside and outside of me were connecting with each other and becoming one and the same. I felt like I was getting back in touch with my true self. This process had silenced the battle going on within me, the one that made me struggle to maintain my sense of self on a daily basis. The only difference now was I didn't struggle with being me. I just was, and just when I thought everything was so good in my world, a blessing and reward was coming for all my hard work. Something I thought I was not prepared for. Something that had eluded me for so long, but that I had always wished I could feel

Love.

I was at a really good place, and I was tapping into so many aspects of myself that I knew were there but could not touch before.

The day my luck changed took me by surprise, and I definitely didn't see it coming. It was late in the day on Saturday, July 21. I know this, because I had a comedy gig that night at the Stirling Festival Theatre. Months ago, I was blessed to connect with a local comedian, Timmy Boyle, who had moved here from Toronto and I

365 Days Single

had always loved to make people laugh. So that's how that connection started. When we connected, he offered me a few minutes at one of his shows. Another time, he offered me a few more minutes. Then I got a couple of other gigs after that and he began to mentor me. I find comedy a perfect fit for my sarcasm and dark humour, and I use it as an outlet to make myself and others laugh. Laughter with or at me has the same effects inside me. I love it. Laughter is the best medicine, and it has helped me through some really tough times.

Anyway, I digress. On the eve of my fourth gig in the past few months, I was lying on my bed reworking some of my material when out of the blue, I thought, I need some kind of shtick. Something that would identify me in the comedian world. I debated about what I should do. I didn't want to wear the same clothes I had already worn. Then it dawned on me, I needed a T-shirt that said something funny. I got up from my bed, hours before my gig, and decided I would go to the local Winners to find such a T-shirt.

When I arrived at the mall, I had no idea what was waiting for me or should I say, who. I walked in, milled through the round racks before heading to the wall rack which had endless T-shirts on it. I still don't understand why the small shirts are six feet off the ground. I am only five foot four and a half (wink) and are all small people 6 feet and over? No. At least I am not. Nonetheless, I started sifting through the wall rack from right to left and near the very end the rack I found the perfect shirt. It was a soft coral colour and it said, *Alcohol You Later*. Perfect!

Since most of my stories were about love, it was too funny to pass up. I pulled the T-shirt off the rack, smiled at its perfectness, and stepped to my left to head to the cash and *wham*! I ran right into a tall, handsome guy who was heading from the back of the store to the front, cutting through the ladies' section to get to the front, and he seemed in a hurry.

"O-oh, excuse me," I stammered.

"No, excuse me," he said in a deep, sensual voice.

Totally caught off guard, I stared into his eyes and immediately felt this powerful magnetic force draw me toward him. He smiled and continued on to the cash, and I was left standing there wondering which way to go. I had what I came to get and felt that I couldn't check out with him standing there.

Disorientation swam over me. I wandered over to the beauty section, which was at least in the right direction. I could still see him. He was cashing out as I looked around at the products, searching for something to pick something up. I'd read an article about Meaghan Markle and how she keeps her curly hair straight with keratin products, so I picked up a conditioner and hairspray loaded with it and headed to cash. He was still there talking to the woman, and I was waiting my turn at the front of the line. He was strikingly handsome. The polite mannerisms he displayed as he spoke to the cashier impressed me. He oozed confidence in every movement he made.

"Next," the cashier said, taking me out of my transcendental state.

As I waited to pay, I could feel him there, and the churning of butterflies danced in my belly. With his transaction completed, he left the store and headed toward the Booster Juice booth just outside the doors. The mystery man had gone about his business. Disappointment rolled over me, and I strolled through the mall, trying to convince the fluttering in my tummy to settle down.

All of a sudden, I could see him walking in the same direction as me. In fact, he was right behind me. Those blasted butterflies erupted again.

"Excuse me," he said again, and I stopped. I turned around to face him. "You are so gorgeous."

It wasn't the first time a man had said this to me, but as our eyes met, it triggered a rush of heat across my cheeks. I was charmed immediately, not by his words. It was the way he spoke them and how he looked at me.

All I could say was, "Thank you." I would normally, just say thank you and walk away, but something inside me sparked.

"You are not from around here, are you?" I inquired.

"No," he said, "I am from Ottawa." That made sense to me, because I think I would have remembered seeing this man somewhere.

"What's your name?"

"Ryan." The name rolled off his tongue like magic. It suited him.

"I'm Orlena," I offered.

"I know who you are," he replied and smiled.

"How?" I was intrigued.

Ryan explained that he lived in Ottawa but was originally from here and knew met me years ago briefly at a public place. After further chatting, I found out he was a friend of mine's older brother. I had no idea my friend had an older brother, since he'd never mentioned him to me.

Friendly, charming banter ensued and I was captivated. We exchanged phone numbers and agreed to connect later. With that, we left each other and I went to my car and quickly called my friend to ask why he never told me he had an older brother and tell him I had just met him. It was a wow moment for me, as it all began to settle in at how much I liked this guy from our brief encounter.

My friend joked, "I guess I'll see you at Thanksgiving, then!" We both laughed, and I hung up and texted Ryan.

It was after two in the afternoon when I met him. A moment that would change my life. A simple act of buying a T-shirt had become something so significant. A thought I had from out of the blue, to get up and go to the store, to be there at the precise moment that he was there trying to exchange something without a receipt. He had to come back the next day with a receipt to do that.

All the "what ifs" come into play when you meet someone who feels so important to you so quickly. What if I hadn't gotten up? What if I hadn't listened to that voice inside my head telling me to go there? But, I did listen to myself, and I responded to it. Something I had forgotten to do over the years. Listen to the voice inside. My life had become so noisy, I could not hear it before. Times prior, if I did hear it, it would be overshadowed by doubtful thoughts. That moment in the mall, changed me, though. I was open to my feelings, I had my fear in check, I was conscious, mindful, and felt ready for anything and that anything was someone, Ryan.

What would transpire over the next two weeks was two people coming to the realization that what they felt the moment they met was in fact an instant connection, one we later came to describe as love at first sight. We didn't know it then, yet, over the weeks and months that followed, it culminated into what we couldn't overlook or explain. The week after we met, I was at my girlfriend's cottage and had planned to not return till Monday, but my Oma's goddaughter had emailed me last minute and told me that she was holding a mini celebration for her son who had recently married an

365 Days Single

American guy.

    She was hosting it in Cobourg, which was close to the cottage, so I arranged my plans to leave the cottage early to attend the event. This left me with Monday off with no plans. I had been communicating with Ryan this whole time through long phone calls and some text messages, and we were steadily becoming fonder of each other.

    When I told him I was off Monday and would be coming back to Belleville after the celebration, he told me he was there again that weekend and asked if I would like to come to Ottawa with him for a few days. The arrangement was effortless. We spent two wonderful days together. The two of us alone in his truck for the three-hour drive to Ottawa, really had the energy bouncing around between us. We talked about anything and everything. As we drove, I never even flinched at the idea of not having my own vehicle so I could leave if I needed or wanted to. This was a new experience. Happily releasing my need to be in control of my destination. It never occurred to me at all. It was not even in my mind.

    Once we were at his place alone with each other, the energy started to really pick up between us. Our time together was spent eating, laughing, sharing stories, and exploring a level of intimacy I never thought myself capable of. We meshed in every way, and what made it even more euphoric was the fact that I wasn't afraid, not even a little bit. There were no moments of doubt or skepticism; I wasn't hypervigilant to search for little things to get my guard up. It was a beautiful experience to be in the moment, utterly and completely.

    As I evaluate this precious moment, I can see how our connection is so deep and powerful. I'd never felt anything like it before. Why? Because I was only half feeling everything before with my guard up and shield handy at all times. Since the past year, I had been doing so much work on me, listening to my inner voice and healing a heart that had been broken for so long that, in the warmth of his embrace and his intense gaze, I began to feel loved. A love that I wanted for so long but was not brave enough to let in was finally seeping in. Something in me changed over those two days.

When he drove me back, the hours of travel just flew by like no time had passed. He owned a construction business and with my own work, the next step of making time was a challenge we gladly met. Initially, neither of us was looking for something serious, but as each moment we spent together would come and go, we found ourselves reaching for more. A long weekend approached, and I had my girlfriend Sonia's husband's surprise fortieth to attend in Toronto on the Sunday and my good friend Cindy's housewarming party in the County on the Friday. I'd intended to attend these events alone, but this weekend was going down in the history books as the most romantic weekend city-hopping from one day to the next.

Ryan initially was hesitant, however, his guard seemed to melt away, and he accompanied me to my friends' housewarming in the County anyway. Stepping out and letting people see us together was huge because I had not done that in the past year and a bit. I had decided at the beginning of my journey that no one I had met was going to spend any time with anyone I knew or be out in public with me because I wasn't looking for anything serious. I was just dating with no expectations. Things evolved daily between Ryan and me.

At the housewarming, there were pictures being taken and these pictures showed the magic that was happening between us. Two people smiling the biggest smiles at each other like we were a couple of teenagers falling in love for the first time. I'd made plans for us to stay at this amazing mini hotel called Cribs on the Creek in Wellington, where I'd had my book launch the year prior. We left the housewarming and went back into Wellington. We decided to stop at the Drake to have a drink or two. Ryan had never been there, and I knew the ambiance on a Friday night would be perfect.

There were so many feelings swirling around between us, it became more and more apparent that something major was happening. It shocked us both that it was happening in such a short period of time, too. As we laughed and sipped drinks at the bar, Ryan confessed how much he was enjoying our time together and how much he liked me. The feeling was mutual, but on a deeper level, I felt something stronger develop. This wasn't just a date or a weekend getaway. This was quality time with someone I genuinely connected with. Teasingly, I tested the waters and said I love you in German, just to see how this felt and sounded for myself. I liked it. He asked what I had said. I said it was German, but I wasn't going to tell him what it was. He logged it into his brain for later, though.

I suggested we walk back to Cribs and enjoy the gas fire pit there and listen to music on our speaker box. Many chairs surrounded the sunken fire pit, and we turned on the music and had fun picking song after song. One song we stood up and began dancing to and Ryan looked down at me with his crystal-blue eyes and said something that radiated into my core.

Ryan told me he was falling in love with me.

In mid-dance, a bride and groom walked by, she with a ring of flowers around her head and the groom in off-white linen. We paused thinking, they were going to join us, but instead they said,

"Don't let us stop your romantic night." They carried on to their room in the building opposite where we were staying. I looked back up at him and wanted to say I loved him at that moment. I wanted to, but I just couldn't let my lips speak the words, and we sat down. Fears that my old demons were about to resurface struck me, and I went silent for a moment, trying to knock the rocks out of my head.

Still in the moment, Ryan hadn't forgotten what I said in German earlier and brought it back up. He took out his phone for Google translate and keyed in what he thought I said.

Ich Liebe Dich.

My throat grew thick as I swallowed back the building emotion. What happened next felt like slow motion. I looked into his incredible eyes and spoke softly. "I love you Ryan."

My pulse thrummed behind my ears; my heart pounded against my chest. My heartbeat was so loud, I'd have sworn the newlyweds could hear it.

Ryan flashed this sweet, boyish smile and said, "I love you, too."

I burst inside, *kaboom*!

If fireworks could have gone off at that moment, they would have, and the night sky began swirling around us ever so slowly. The night enveloped the two of us, and he drew me in for a deep, building, soulful kiss. The connection I'd spent a lifetime craving had finally arrived with three simple words and the touch of our lips. I knew now, in that moment, this was real, for the first time, the love I had spent forever searching for had finally found me. Everything I'd wanted to feel and share with a person for so long was right there in front of me and all around me.

LESSON: My lesson in this final chapter of my 365 day journey, was love. After committing to the most important relationship of my

365 Days Single

life—with myself for an entire year, I spent most of these days rediscovering, healing, growing, and learning about the things that make me, me. I learned about what drives me, what makes me tick, and what could have inevitably broken me, if I hadn't taken the time to pause and shift my focus to better my life. I learned we all have our demons, our pain from the past. It doesn't have to define us, or control us. We have more personal power to make the changes necessary to find peace within ourselves and with our past. I exposed the reasons why I had become a serial monogamist and why it never worked in my favour.

We all develop crutches to hold us up when we feel vulnerable, but these crutches can become our undoing. If we don't strengthen our injuries, how can we get back to functioning at our best? Digging deep and peeling back the toxic layers can be frightening, even terrifying for some. In many cases, it may mean reliving the trauma in order to release it. If we don't believe enough in ourselves to face these things that hurt us, how can we heal?

I learned, in order to be truly open to love, my journey wasn't about simply finding the right guy to connect with. It was about finding myself. About saving that little girl who was traumatized for so many years. It was time to liberate my inner child from the confines of fear and set her free. Over the course of my 365 days of being single, I experienced great loss and sorrow, I addressed old patterns of behaviour and explored my failed attempts at finding love. I overhauled my life and cut away the anchors that were holding me down, and I forgave.

My healing journey has not come to an end; it's only just begun. I know I will continue to stumble across setbacks and challenges along the way. I know there will be days when the past still returns in some form to remind me where I came from. I also know, I'll meet these challenges head on and stare them right in the eye. I will continue to learn, heal, and grow.

As for me and Ryan, our story is just beginning. Our connection is so real and so powerful and what would transpire in the days ahead only cemented the feeling further for us. So much more could be said about the two of us, but what I will say is that we are together and very much in love with plans for a beautiful future together. Something real and unconditional. We accepted each other with toe-curling, undeniable love.

What we feel inside for each other reminds me of a poem from the Guillermo Del Toro's movie *The Shape of Water*. I watched this movie when it came out and in fact Ryan and I watched it together the night before I finished these last few sentences. The poem was originally written by a thirteenth century Persian Sufi mystic poet Rumi, it says at the end of the movie, "*Unable to perceive the shape of You. I find You all around me. Your presence fills my eyes with Your love, It humbles my heart, for You are everywhere.*"